University of Charleston Library
Charleston, WV 25304

Research in
Reading in English as a Second Language

Research in Reading in English as a Second Language

Joanne Devine
Patricia L. Carrell
David E. Eskey
editors

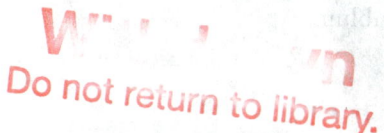

Teachers of English to Speakers of Other Languages

Staff Editors: Julia Frank-McNeil
Juana E. Hopkins
Helen J. Kornblum

Copyright © 1987 by
Teachers of English to Speakers of Other Languages
Washington, D.C.
Printed in the U.S.A.

Copying or further publication of the contents of this work is not permitted without permission of TESOL, except for limited "fair use" for educational, scholarly, and similar purposes as authorized by U.S. Copyright Law, in which case appropriate notice of the source of the work should be given.

Library of Congress Catalog No. 87-050893
ISBN 0-93979130

Table of Contents

Introduction
Patricia L. Carrell   1

The Eclectic Synergy of Methods of Reading Research
Ulla Connor   9

A View of Written Text as Communicative Interaction: Implications for Reading in a Second Language
Patricia L. Carrell   21

Comments on Carrell
Sandra Silberstein   36

The Effect of Context and Culture on Children's L2 Reading: A Review
Margaret S. Steffensen   41

Comments on Steffensen
Liz Hamp-Lyons   55

Reading in a Second Culture
Kate J. Parry   59

Comments on Parry
Mary Lee Field   71

General Language Competence and Adult Second Language Reading
Joanne Devine   73

Comments on Devine
David E. Eskey   86

Does Syntactic Rewriting Affect English for Science and Technology Text Comprehension?
Judith B. Strother and Jan M. Ulijn   89

Comments on Strother and Ulijn
James Coady   101

High-Level Reading in the First and in the Foreign Language: Some Comparative Process Data
Gissi Sarig   105

Comments on Sarig
Fraida Dubin   121

Cognitive Strategy Transfer in Second Language Reading
Keiko Koda   125

Comments on Koda
William Grabe   145

The Relationship Between Nonverbal Schematic Concept Formation and Story Comprehension
Kyle Perkins   151

Comments on Perkins
Andrew D. Cohen   172

ESL Reading Pedagogy: Implications of Schema-Theoretical Research
Mark O. James   175

Conclusion
David E. Eskey   189

Introduction

Research in Reading in English as a Second Language is the outgrowth of the 3rd Annual Colloquium on Research in Reading in a Second Language presented at the 19th Annual TESOL Convention in New York City in April 1985. This anthology contains most of the papers presented at that Colloquium, plus selected additional papers on the topic, which were also presented at the 1985 TESOL Convention.

The Colloquium, which was first presented at the 1983 TESOL Convention in Toronto, organized by Joanne Devine and Ulla Connor, and again at the 1984 TESOL Convention in Houston, organized by Joanne Devine and Patricia L. Carrell, assumed a unique identity at the 1985 Convention under the leadership of Devine, Carrell, and David E. Eskey. Enthusiastic response to the 1983 and 1984 colloquia attested to the widespread interest among the TESOL membership in the development of second language reading proficiency. The 1985 Colloquium sought to continue to provide scholars actively engaged in research in reading in a second language with a forum for reporting their work, exchanging ideas, and suggesting directions for continued research and for pedagogy. It further sought to engage researchers/scholars in meaningful dialogue with practitioners in the audience.

Rather than a random selection of papers on any aspects of research in reading in English as a second language (ESL), the 1985 Colloquium continued to focus on the theme established in the 1984 Colloquium, that of ESL reading as interaction with a text. The basis for this theme is a view of reading as an active process which involves many reader, as well as text, variables in complex interaction. There were eight major presentations at the all-day colloquium, exploring various aspects of this central focus. Five of these eight papers are included in this volume (Connor, Carrell, Steffensen, Devine, and Perkins). The paper by Sarig was to have been presented at the 1985 Colloquium, but last-minute circumstances prevented her from attending. We are pleased that we are able to include her paper.

In addition to the core of papers from the 1985 Colloquium, we have included several other significant contributions on research in reading in English as a second language from the general 1985 TESOL Convention program. These are the papers by Parry, Strother and Ulijn, Koda, and James. The other colloquium participants (Silberstein, Hamp-Lyons, Field, Eskey, Coady, Dubin, Grabe, and Cohen) have provided brief commentaries on and reactions to the papers in this volume, excluding only the Connor and James papers which are largely descriptive.

Although we cannot claim that the papers in this volume exhaustively represent all of the areas of research currently being undertaken in ESL reading, they do reflect the current status of research on reading in English as a second language as represented on the program of the 1985 TESOL Convention. Our purpose in bringing these papers together is to illustrate both the diversity and the richness of that research, as well as to reflect on its common themes. Each of the contributing authors approaches the topic of research in reading in English as a second language from a unique perspective and investigates different aspects of second language reading; however, general themes and common perspectives underlie the papers. It is these common threads which reveal the current state of the art of ESL reading research.

Not surprisingly, the most general theme is the one around which the 1985 Reading Research Colloquium was organized: Reading is a multifaceted, complex, interactive process which involves many subskills and many types of reader, as well as text, variables. Every paper in this volume reflects some aspect of this general theme. No longer can reading in a second language (or reading in general, for that matter) be viewed as a passive process. Nor is reading simply an active process; rather, efficient and effective reading requires a true interaction between reader and text. No longer can reading be viewed as a simple mapping of (oral) language skills into another medium. No longer can second language reading be viewed as a simple transfer of first language reading abilities to a second language setting. No longer is the text or even a text analysis sufficient to explain reading difficulties; everything about the reader and the reader's background, especially culture-specific knowledge and experiences, is relevant to successful reading and reading comprehension. In one way or another, all of the papers in this volume reflect this general theme.

Within this general theme, a number of more specific subthemes run through the papers in this volume. One of the more prevalent subthemes is the view that if reading is an interactive process between reader and text, then this necessitates an examination of both top-down (conceptually driven) and bottom-up (input/data driven) processes and their interplay. Furthermore, for the interaction between reader and text to be studied, the richness of both reader and text variables must all be considered. The Carrell and James papers in the volume are particularly representative of this theme. (Each of the contributed papers and the associated discussant's comments are described in the second part of this introduction.)

A second subtheme is the conviction that, because of the complexity of the reading process, a wide variety of research methods is necessary to tap various aspects of that complex process. Researchers are exploring a variety of methods that will allow us to tap the process more or less directly: via think-aloud protocols, interview and immediate-introspection techniques, ethnographic methods, in addition to miscue analyses and recall procedures.

Connor's paper on research methods, as well as Parry's and Sarig's papers, reflect this theme most strongly.

A third major subtheme is recognition of the important role played by cultural background factors. Several papers explore this theme directly, examining how the cultural knowledge possessed by the reader interacts with that presumed by the text. Steffensen's and Parry's papers, in particular, take this theme as their point of departure.

Another set of subthemes concerns the extent to which language skills, that is, linguistic proficiency in the second language, may be distinct from and related to other skills and proficiencies which make up successful reading in English as a second language (i.e., reading skills, background knowledge). This theme, which has been an issue in second language reading research since the late 1970s (Cziko, 1978; Clarke, 1979, 1980) is further explored and expanded in several of the papers in this volume, most notably those by Devine, Strother and Ulijn, Perkins, and James. Furthermore, given that linguistic proficiency in the second language plays a significant role in second language reading, several papers explore the relative importance of various aspects of that linguistic proficiency, especially the relative importance of lexical versus grammatical proficiency. This subtheme is a central focus of both the Strother and Ulijn, and Devine papers.

A final common subtheme is the relationship between reading in a first or native language and reading in a second language, specifically in English as the second language. Exploring both sides of this relationship involves not only those themes mentioned above concerning linguistic proficiency in the second language and issues concerning individual differences in the reading process, but also requires researchers to face questions about possible universals in the reading process, the role of general cognitive strategies and cognitive styles, and the relationship of reading to other cognitive skills and abilities, including those which are nonverbal. Particularly reflective of this cognitive theme are the contributions by Sarig, Koda, and Perkins.

The volume begins with Ulla Connor's "The Eclectic Synergy of Methods of Reading Research." This paper, which was the culminating and summarizing paper from the 1985 Colloquium, was chosen to lead this volume because it sets the stage for the types of research methods represented in the other papers. Connor's survey of different types of methods used in both first and second language reading research includes experimental, descriptive, and ethnographic research. The survey also includes the methodologies of miscue analysis, interviews, and think-aloud protocols, as well as training studies.

The next paper, Patricia L. Carrell's "A View of Written Text as Communicative Interaction," explains and espouses the view of written text as communicative interaction of de Beaugrande (1980). After establishing second language reading as an interactive process and briefly reviewing the recent history of approaches to ESL reading, Carrell presents a strong argument for the relevance of de Beaugrande and Dressler's (1981) seven principles of textuality for interactive approaches to second language reading. Sandra Silberstein's comments on Carrell's paper suggest additional sources of interactive views of reading, with particularly strong emphasis on the role of the reader from three different strains of literary criticism: reader response theory, Marxist literary theory, and feminist film criticism.

Margaret S. Steffensen's position paper, "The Effect of Context and Culture on Children's L2 Reading: A Review," presents the current state of the art of research in children's reading, focusing specifically on the lack of relevant research on the role of cultural background knowledge and its effects on children's reading. She suggests several reasons for the relative inattention this phenomenon has received in children's second language (L2) reading research. Steffensen advocates the use of Fillmore's (1981) interview method, also discussed in Connor's paper, as an effective method in assessing the effects of cultural background knowledge on children's L2 reading. Liz Hamp-Lyons' comments on Steffensen's paper explore a number of pedagogical and research implications raised by the research which Steffensen reviews. For example, what can or should the classroom teacher do when there is a conflict between the reader's background knowledge and the information in the text? Might children, if they do indeed have less well-developed cultural schemata, be more receptive to learning foreign schemata?

Kate Parry's "Reading in a Second Culture" is linked to the Steffensen paper by its focus on the cultural dimensions of second language reading. Using ethnographic research methods (also discussed in Connor's introductory paper), Parry investigates Nigerian students' difficulties in understanding written English. Her findings suggest a complex interaction of a number of lexical, syntactic, rhetorical, and schematic factors causing comprehension problems. Mary Lee Field's comments serve to further develop a recurring theme in Parry's paper: the differences between literate cultures and oral cultures. Field discusses the double bind many groups of ESL readers encounter: having to read in a second (or even third) language, in addition to having to function according to the expectations of a literate culture rather than an oral one.

Joanne Devine's paper, "General Language Competence and Adult Second Language Reading," reports results from an ongoing study exploring the relationship between various measures of language proficiency and of reading strategies, the latter measured by oral reading miscue analysis. Although her results generally reaffirm the relationship between general ESL proficiency and reading performance (Clarke, 1979, 1980; Cziko, 1978, 1980; Hudson, 1982), specific results with grammar and vocabulary subscores suggest that if language instruction is to have a positive impact on reading ability, such instruction should be integrative and holistic, not concentrated on specific subskills. David E. Eskey comments that Devine's results support an interactive view of reading in which successful readers make use of cues at all levels—graphophonic to schematic. Eskey further comments on the implications of Devine's findings concerning holistic and integrative learning by articulating a central paradox facing those of us who would turn theory into pedagogical practice: Much of what must be learned apparently cannot be taught.

Judith B. Strother and Jan Ulijn's paper, "Does Syntactic Rewriting Affect EST Text Comprehension?" is also concerned with the potentially different roles of grammar and vocabulary in second language reading. It summarizes an empirical study of the relationship between syntactic rewriting (simplification) and reading in English for science and technology (EST). Their findings suggest that concentration on lexical skills and lexical rewriting may increase learning from texts and text readability, respectively. Therefore, the focus of reading pedagogy for advanced students, particularly EST students, should be on the development of conceptual and lexical skills. James Coady comments on two aspects of Strother and Ulijn's paper: their research methodology and syntactic simplification. In his comments on their research methodology, Coady touches on the important issue of research which is based on the null hypothesis, that is, when researchers set out to prove there is no difference, no effect, no relationship. In his comments on syntactic simplification, Coady raises questions about the relationships among vocabulary, syntactic simplification, and the meaningfulness of text.

Gissi Sarig's paper, "High-Level Reading in the First and in the Foreign Language: Some Comparative Process Data," reports an empirical study using think-aloud and immediate-introspection techniques to investigate the relationship between first (Hebrew) and second (English) language reading. Results of her study show first and second language reading to be a highly individual process. Further, there appears to be a high degree of overlap between first and second language high-level reading strategies, suggesting that reading instruction in the first language should carry over positively to second language reading. Fraida Dubin's comments highlight the importance of mentalistic methods, such as the think-aloud and introspection techniques used by Sarig, and the significance of Sarig's findings concerning the transfer of reading strategies from native to second language reading. Dubin also comments on the potential pedagogical relevance of Sarig's taxonomy of learner's strategies. Examination of Sarig's strategies may help materials developers prepare more systematic and more meaningful reading activities geared to particular strategy intervention.

Keiko Koda's paper investigates the question of "Cognitive Strategy Transfer in Second Language Reading" at the level of orthographic/phonological systems. In an empirical study of Japanese readers' transfer of a logographic-lexical orthographic strategy to reading in English with an alphabetic-phonological orthography, Koda found evidence that the Japanese readers transfer their native logographic reading strategy to reading in ESL. They differ, however, from native speakers of English in the effects of differences in phonological accessibility versus inaccessibility. The amount of phonological recoding the Japanese readers engage in to decipher the English orthographic system varies from that of native English speakers. However, Koda found evidence of some phonological recoding even among beginning ESL students and speculates, therefore, that the orthographically-based transfer phenomenon will be less strong as learners improve their oral ESL proficiency. Critically questioning some of the assumptions underlying Koda's study, William Grabe explores a number of issues raised by Koda's paper. Grabe's close critique provides additional insights into issues involved in studying cognitive strategy transfer.

Kyle Perkins' paper, "The Relationship between Nonverbal Schematic Concept Formation and Story Comprehension," reports an empirical study linking readers' abilities in a nonverbal domain to story comprehension in ESL. Perkins claims a significant relationship between ability to nonverbally schematize and performance on ESL reading comprehension questions. This research raises the questions: Are some ESL readers better (nonverbal) schematizers than others, and, if so, how does this ability affect ESL reading? Loosely related to other research on narrative schemata, Perkins' research is part of the body of research currently posing questions about ESL readers' relevant formal schemata (cf. Carrell, 1984a, 1984b; Hinds, 1983). Andrew Cohen's comments on Perkins' paper caution against relying too heavily on nonverbal tasks, such as Perkins' schematic concept formation task, as predictors of reading ability. Among other things, Cohen notes that studies have failed to yield high correlations between nonverbal cognitive processing tasks and language processing tasks. In fact, Perkins' nonverbal task failed to relate to story schematic categories within the reading-question answering task, and finally, Cohen concludes that question-answering tasks have their own shortcomings. Cohen agrees with Perkins that more research in this area is indicated in order to better understand Perkins' findings.

The volume concludes with Mark James' paper, "ESL Reading Pedagogy: Implications of Schema-Theoretical Research." Like Perkins, James is concerned with schema theory in ESL reading. As the title indicates, the paper focuses on pedagogical implications of schema theory for ESL reading classrooms. After a brief introduction and review of schema theory and the distinction among linguistic, content, and formal schema (cf. Carrell, 1983), James suggests classroom implications in terms of reading material, prereading activities, and postreading activities. James' suggestions are closely akin to similar suggestions previously proposed by Carrell (Carrell & Eisterhold, 1983; Carrell, 1984c, 1984d).

Thus, the papers collected in this volume, together with discussants' comments, represent not only individual pieces of research on specific topics, but also major contributions to the general state of our knowledge about reading in English as a second language in terms of the general themes outlined at the beginning of this introduction.

The editors wish to thank all the contributors, both authors and discussants, for their cooperation in making this volume possible. We further wish to thank H. Douglas Brown, Chair of the TESOL Publications Committee (1985), and two anonymous reviewers for their constructive suggestions in editing this volume.

Patricia L. Carrell

References

de Beaugrande, R. (1980). *Test, discourse, and process*. Norwood, NJ: Ablex.
de Beaugrande, R., & Dressler, W. (1981). *Introduction to text linquistics*. London: Longman.
Carrell, P. L. (1983). Some issues in studying the role of schemata, or background knowledge in second language comprehension. *Reading in a Foreign Language, 1*, 81-92.
Carrell, P. L. (1984a). Evidence of a formal schema in second language comprehension. *Language Learning, 34*, 87-112.
Carrell, P. L. (1984b). The effects of rhetorical organization on ESL readers. *TESOL Quarterly, 18*, 441-469.
Carrell, P. L. (1984c). Schema theory and ESL reading: Classroom implications and applications. *Modern Language Journal, 68*, 332-343.
Carrell, P. L. (1984d, October). Interactive text processing: Implications for ESL reading classrooms. Paper presented at the 4th Annual Midwest Regional TESOL Meeting, Cincinnati, OH.
Carrell, P. L., & Eisterhold, J. C. (1983). Schema theory and ESL reading pedagogy. *TESOL Quarterly, 17*, 553-573.
Clarke, M. A. (1979). Reading in Spanish and English: Evidence from adult ESL students. *Language Learning, 29*, 121-150.
Clarke, M. A. (1980). The short-circuit hypothesis of ESL reading - or when language competence interferes with reading performance. *Modern Language Journal, 64*, 203-209.
Cziko, G. A. (1978). Differences in first- and second-language reading: The use of syntactic, semantic and discourse constraints. *Canadian Modern Language Review, 34*, 473-489.
Cziko, G. A. (1980). Language competence and reading strategies: A comparison of first- and second-language oral reading errors. *Language Learning, 30*, 101-116.
Fillmore, C. J. (1981). Ideal readers and real readers. In D. Tannen (Ed.), *Analyzing discourse: Text and talk* (pp. 248-270). Washington, DC: Georgetown University.
Hinds, J. L. (1983) Contrastive rhetoric: Japanese and English. *Text, 3*, 183-195.
Hudson, T. (1982). The effects of induced schemata on the "short circuit" in L2 reading: Non-decoding factors in L2 reading performance. *Language Learning, 32*, 1-31.

The Eclectic Synergy of Methods of Reading Research

Ulla Connor

Indiana University at Indianapolis

The Eclectic Synergy of Methods of Reading Research

Reading research in both first and second language uses multiple methods to reach a new understanding of the nature of reading, its contexts, and developmental stages. The use of multiple methods has evolved largely from the academic backgrounds of those who became interested in reading problems. Psychologists have favored experimental studies. On the other hand, linguists have advocated case studies and textual studies, while anthropologists and sociolinguists have introduced ethnographies. This multimodality can be problematic, as judgments about a piece of scholarship are sometimes mistaken because the nature of the research method is misunderstood. Other times, a new theory is criticized for methods that do not provide rigorous knowledge. In this paper two methods of empirical research will be addressed, experimental and descriptive. My claim is that the multimodality of reading research is an asset which provides researchers multiple methods to investigate their research problems. I will highlight areas in need of research in English as a second language based upon comparisons with native English reading research.

Experimental Research

Experimental and Quasi-Experimental Design

Experimental research is highly valued in the social sciences because it can establish cause-and-effect relationships. To test their hypotheses, researchers divide the environment into treatment and control groups, administer treatments, and assess the results with measurement instruments that, it is hoped, are valid and reliable. There are two types of experimental research which vary in the extent of control: the true experiment and the quasi-experiment. In true experiments, subjects are assigned to groups randomly, which permits the researcher to consider the groups equal. Then, if the treatment group performs significantly better, the treatment is said to have caused the difference. In quasi-experiments, because the groups have not been randomized, more sophisticated statistical procedures must be used to establish that the treatment has made a difference in the results. The strength of the claim for cause and effect still lies on the validity of the measurements used.

There have been several objections to some experimental studies. Until now many reading studies have relied on standardized test scores or scores on a small number of questions following a reading passage; the validity of these measures has been questioned by Fillmore (1981) and Connor (1985). Others have pointed out that the hypotheses are not always based on real issues, or that the right questions might not have been asked (Bloom & Green, 1984). One final objection to experimental research is that some researchers within that mode report the results of statistical tests but fail to discuss the results any further (Fasold, 1982).

Training Studies

Perhaps because of the many difficulties related to designing field experiments (a classroom), few research studies have examined variables in teaching reading comprehension to ESL students. In first language (L1), however, a fairly extensive body of research exists in instructional intervention. In Table 1, these studies are classified by the type of pedagogical activity:

Table 1. Summary of Training Studies for Teaching Reading Comprehension

Types of Training	L1 studies *	L2 studies
Prereading Activities		
Building background knowledge		
Preteaching vocabulary	x	Johnson (1982)
Enriching background knowledge	x	Carrell (1984a, 1984b)
Activating background knowledge	x	—
Advancing organizers	x	—
Objectives	x	—
Pretests or prequestions	x	—
Pictures and titles	x	—
Guided Reading Activities		
Inducing imagery	x	—
Inserted questions	x	—
Self-questioning	x	—
Directed reading activity	x	—
Post-Reading Activities		
Post questioning	x	—
Feedback	x	—
Group and class discussion	x	—

* "x" indicates that numerous studies exist. See Tierney and Cunningham (1984) for a comprehensive review of the studies.

prereading activities, guided reading activities, and postreading activities. This useful trichotomy distinguishes among the strategies upon which a pedagogical method is based. The distinctions then focus on: (a) building background knowledge and activating it before reading, (b) guiding reader/text interactions during the reading, and (c) providing review and feedback after reading. The figure provides more detailed categories of study and sample references for ESL. (For a thorough review of L1 training studies with a useful discussion of future research suggestions, see Tierney & Cunningham, 1984).

Training studies of ESL reading are few, as column 3 of Table 1 indicates; three published studies include Johnson (1982) and Carrell (1984a, 1984b). Johnson investigated the effects on reading comprehension of building background knowledge by teaching target vocabulary words to the students in the treatment group using three different teaching strategies (studying of definitions, words glossed in the passage, and studying definitions coupled with words glossed). Johnson found that the exposure to meanings of the target vocabulary words did not have a significant effect on reading comprehension by any of the treatments; L1 research also shows conflicting evidence about the benefits of introducing new word meanings before having students read. The consensus in L1 is that teaching vocabulary is probably only justified when just one or two crucial words are taught. Other training studies in ESL are Carrell's series of studies on the teaching of Meyer's major expository discourse types to ESL students: collection of descriptions, causation, problem/solution, and comparison. The instructional intervention in Carrell's research resulted in better recognition and use of the trained discourse types, as well as increased amount of recalled information.

The reported results and discussions of L1 training studies can offer useful guidance for ESL teachers and researchers. However, not all evidence supports success in teaching the listed activities. For example, the question of the effect of pictures and titles on reading comprehension is controversial. Samuels (1970), Thomas (1978), and Marr (1979) have all shown that pictures fail to have a facilitative effect on learning. In contrast, a growing number of studies have found evidence to the contrary (e.g., Guttman, Levin, & Pressley, 1977; Levin & Lesgold, 1978). A number of questions remain to be answered: How might the information in the pictures be measured? What kind of information should be represented in the pictures?

Descriptive Research

Descriptive studies entail observation of phenomena and analysis of data, but they do not include manipulation or restructuring of the situation or environment under scrutiny. The status of this kind of empirical research varies from field to field. Some behavioral and social scientists view it as prescientific research, which should be done when one is looking for hypotheses to test. Other fields, however, such as anthropology and sociolinguistics, give it a high status. In L1 reading research, several researchers are calling for more descriptive studies (Guthrie & Hall, 1984).

There is a wealth of second language research studies that have used a descriptive method. Table 2 lists the types and sample studies. The studies are briefly described; in those cases where no L2 studies exist, references to exemplary L1 research will be made.

Miscue Analysis

One of the most popular methods in reading research using the case study mode has been that of reading miscue analysis (Goodman, 1969). Miscue analysis focuses on oral reading performance of individual readers. The analysis of the oral reading is linguistically based; graphemic, phonemic, semantic, and syntactic miscues are recorded and analyzed. Several ESL reading miscue analysis studies have been conducted (Rigg, 1977; Devine, 1980;

Table 2. Summary of In-depth Descriptive Studies

Type of Method	L1 studies *	L2 studies
Miscue Analysis	x	Rigg (1977) Devine (1980, 1981) Connor (1981)
"Think-aloud"	—	Hosenfield (1977) Hosenfield and Cohen (1981)
Fillmore Interview Method	x	Connor (1985) Steffensen (1980)
Computerized On-line Method	x	—
Longitudinal Case Studies	x	Briggs (1984)
Ethnographic Research	x	(see Guthrie and Hall, 1984)
Metacognitive Studies	x	(see Baker and Brown, 1984)

* "x" indicates that numerous studies exist. See Pearson, Barr, Kamil, and Mosenthal (1984) for comprehensive reviews.

Connor, 1981). There is no doubt that the miscue analysis research has added to the knowledge of the reading process of ESL readers and has confirmed the notion that ESL readers, like first language readers, do not rely on a word as a unit but take into account the context and the syntactic, phonological, and semantic cues in a text.

Reading miscue analysis is recognized as a valuable dimension in diagnosing individual reading problems, but its role as a research method is being questioned. Allington (1984) provides a detailed up-to-date review of the criticisms of miscue analysis as a research method. The following are the most serious weaknesses:

1. No empirical validation of the relative effectiveness of strategies by different readers reading texts of varying levels.
2. The assumption that a fully developed set of language skills comes into play during the reading process; poor readers in their first language have been found to experience a delay in certain language abilities, which applied to ESL readers' English language skills.
3. The assumption that oral and silent reading represents a unitary phenomenon.
4. Problems with the readability of coding procedures.

The Think-Aloud Method

To find out the processes by which learners in a second language read and to help them acquire new reading strategies, Hosenfeld has conducted several studies using a technique called *thinking aloud.* The technique requires students to read a passage and think aloud as they are doing it, either in the second or first language. Hosenfeld's first study (1977) investigated how successful and unsuccessful students (a total of 40) go about assigning meaning to the printed text. Hosenfeld has also conducted research with a single second language reader for the purpose of documenting both reading behavior and the student's ability to acquire new reading strategies. To my knowledge, this technique has not been used in published research besides the studies by Hosenfeld and Cohen, reviewed in *Language Learning* (Cohen & Hosenfeld, 1981). The technique has proved to be useful, however, in at least two recent dissertations on ESL reading: Addison's (1983) award-winning dissertation on ESL students and secondary school science texts and McCagg's (1984) dissertation on inferencing by Japanese ESL readers. In both these studies, the think-aloud technique provided additional information about the strategies ESL learners use to gather information from a text—information not available through traditional comprehension checks, suggesting the eclectic synergy of methods of reading research.

The Fillmore Interview Method

This method was developed by Charles Fillmore (1981) to examine interactive processes in reading among native English-speaking children, but the method has been adopted by researchers to gain insights into the reading behaviors of ESL learners (Connor, 1985; Steffensen, 1981). Fillmore was interested in how young readers construct an understanding of reading passages, and how this understanding can be used to find best answers to standardized reading comprehension questions. An important aspect of Fillmore's model is the abstract concept of the ideal reader and the real reader. The ideal reader is one "who sees the connections, creates the expectations, performs the inferences, and asks the questions" (Fillmore, 1981, p. 252) that the writer has intended. In real life, of course, real readers seldom measure up to the ideal reader.

The actual methodology is based on an assumption that a reader sees a reading passage one segment at a time, while a researcher sees it as a whole. Fillmore conducted reading interviews with elementary school children by showing the reader one clause-length segment of a reading test at a time. The children were asked to answer questions and make predictions after they had read each segment. The questions the interviewer asks are related to content domain schemata, text domain schemata, genre schemata, and point of view. Fillmore admits that exact questions vary somewhat from one interview situation to another. The role of the interviewer cannot be overemphasized in maintaining consistency from one interview to another.

Computerized On-Line Methods

The study of eye movements is an old line of research in reading comprehension and is being revitalized in L1 reading. Psychologists have been intrigued for a long time with model building based upon observations of eye movements during reading (Huey, 1908; Gibson & Levin, 1975; Just & Carpenter, 1980, 1984). Studies have shown that good readers modify their eye movements when faced with difficult material and adapt them accordingly when reading for the general idea versus detailed information. A new, improved method was proposed by Ingvar Lundberg (1984). Instead of measuring the physical movement of the eye, Lundberg avoided the criticism that the eye was not a clear picture of the mind by using what he calls a "text-window." The text-window sheds light on a variable length of text, and the reader can adjust the speed of the text-window both forward and backward. The method seems to have validity in efforts to learn about strategies readers use in reading. In light of easy availability of microcomputers, it may become a popular method of research.

Longitudinal Case Study

More research is needed to gather information about the multitude of background variables that enter into a successful second-language reading. One of the few longitudinal case studies available is Sarah Briggs' (1984) dissertation from Indiana University in Bloomington. Briggs investigated six graduate ESL students, collecting information through interviews, administration of reading tests, and systematic observations of the subjects' reading over several months. The results of her inquiry indicated that all the ESL readers were similar in some ways to readers of English as L1. Similarities and differences varied from case to case, as could be expected. All read much more slowly than native speakers, but all were able to be successful in their course readings.

Ethnographic Research[1]

Ethnographic methods in L1 reading research have included school and classroom observation (Cook-Gumperz, Gumperz, & Simons, 1981; McDermott, 1976) and interviews with key informants after videotaping of classes (Mehan, 1979), or interviews with readers who had taken a reading test (Cicourel, 1974; Bauman, 1982). In ESL, ethnographic methods were well accepted for the study of spoken language behavior, as evidenced by the surge of publications in classroom-centered research. Ethnographic research in ESL reading, however, seems virgin territory.

Metacognitive Studies

The premise of this paper has been that multimodality of methods of research is an asset. Having shown that the labels "experimental" or "descriptive" could be used to describe many of the studies mentioned, several of the studies have used multiple methods to gain deeper insights into L2 reading behavior. A good example of the necessity of the multimodality of methods is one area of study that in the last 5 years has gained unforeseen popularity: the study of metacognition.

Psychologists involved in L1 research have investigated the following under the rubric of metacognition: (a) readers' knowledge of their own cognitive resources and their compatibility with the reading situation, (b) self-regulatory mechanisms used by an active learner during an attempt to solve a problem, and (c) development and use of compensatory strategies for either reading for meaning or reading for remembering. Metacognitive studies have used a variety of methods as discussed in detail by Baker and Brown (1984): interview investigations, self-correction during reading, the cloze technique, several on-line measures, self-reports during reading, retrospective reports and recall protocols, and analysis of macrorules for comprehension and retention. Many of these methods resemble the ones reviewed under descriptive studies (e.g., think-aloud). The difference between the earlier mentioned ESL studies and L1 metacognition studies is that the latter typically include more testable hypotheses, thus combining experimental and descriptive methods to a greater degree than is usual in ESL reading research. This feature again may be explained by the backgrounds (psychology) of the researchers of metacognition.

Conclusion

This review of methods of reading research shows that in ESL reading research, there is indeed an eclectic synergy of methods. There are studies in all the major methodological categories, and the studies employ multiple methods. In light of L1 research directions, it is clear that ESL empirical studies show a preference for descriptive methods over experimental studies. This is probably attributable to the fact that many ESL researchers have linguistic backgrounds rather than training in quantitative methods. There are exceptions, of course, as illustrated in Table 1.

Since descriptive studies have generated a sufficient number of theories of reading processes, I would recommend that more experiments be conducted to test these theories. Experimental research should not prevent the use of descriptive methods to augment the design and analyses. It is only through this increased, more balanced set of studies, that we can build up a comprehensive theory of the ESL reading process.

References

Addison, A. A. (1983). *A discourse analysis of secondary school science textbooks with a comparison of text features and reading comprehension for native and non-native English-speaking students.* Unpublished doctoral dissertation, Georgetown University, Washington, DC.

Allington, R. (1984). Oral reading. In P. D. Pearson, R. Barr, M. L. Kamil, & P. Mosenthal (Eds.), *Handbook of reading research* (pp. 829-864). New York: Longman.

Baker, L. & Brown, A. L. (1984). Metacognitive skills and reading, In P. O. Pearson, R. Barr, M. L. Kamil, & P. Mosenthal (Eds.), *Handbook of reading research* (pp. 91-110). New York: Longman.

Bauman, R. F. (1972). An ethnographic framework for the investigation of communicative behavior. In R. Abrahams & R. Troike (Eds.), *Language and cultural diversity in American education* (pp. 154-166). Englewood Cliffs, NJ: Prentice Hall.

Bloom, D., & Green, J. (1984). Directions in the sociolinguistic study of reading. In P. D. Pearson, R. Barr, M. L. Kamil, & P. Mosenthal (Eds.), *Handbook of reading research* (pp. 395-422). New York: Longman.

Briggs, S. (1984). *Proficient reading in English as a second language: Six case studies of graduate students at an American university.* Unpublished doctoral dissertation, Indiana University, Bloomington.
Carrell, P. L. (1984a, March). Facilitating reading comprehension by teaching text structure: what the research shows. Paper presented at the 18th Annual TESOL Convention, Houston, TX.
Carrell, P. L. (1984b, August). Reading comprehension and the rhetorical organization of text. Paper presented at the 7th World Congress of the International Association of Applied Linguistics, Brussels.
Cicourel, A. V. (1974). *Cognitive sociology.* New York: Free Press.
Cohen, A. D., & Hosenfeld, C. (1981). Some uses of mentalistic data in second language research. *Language Learning, 31,* 285-314.
Connor, U. (1981). The application of reading miscue analysis to diagnosis of English as a second language learners' reading skills. In C. W. Twyford, W. Diehl, & K. Feathers (Eds.), *Reading English as a second language: Moving from theory* (pp. 47-55). Bloomington: Indiana University.
Connor, U. (1985). In search of the ideal bilingual reader using a new interview research method. Unpublished manuscript. Indiana University, Indianapolis.
Cook-Gumperz, J., Gumperz, J. T., & Simons, H. (1981). *School home ethnography project* (Final Report). Washington, DC: National Institute of Education.
Devine, J. (1980). *Developmental patterns in native and non-native reading acquisition.* Unpublished doctoral dissertation, Michigan State University, East Lansing.
Devine, J. (1981). Developmental patterns in native and non-native reading acquisition. In S. Hudelson (Ed.), *Learning to read in different languages.* Washington, DC: Center for Applied Linguistics.
Fasold, R. (1983). [Course notes for statistics for Linguists]. Washington, DC: Georgetown University.
Fillmore, C. (1981). Ideal readers and real readers. In Deborah Tannen (Ed.), *Analyzing discourse: Text and talk.* Washington DC: Georgetown University.
Gibson, E. J., & Levin, H. (1975). *The psychology of reading.* Cambridge, MA: MIT Press.
Goodman, K. S. (1969). Analysis of reading miscues: Applied psycholinguistics. *Reading Research Quarterly, 5,* 9-30.
Guthrie, L. F., & Hall, W. S. (1984). Ethnographic approaches to reading research. In P. D. Pearson, R. Barr, M. L. Kamil, P. Mosenthal (Eds.), *Handbook of reading research* (pp. 91-110). New York: Longman.
Guttman, J., Levin, J. R., & Pressley, M. (1977). Pictures, partial pictures, and young children's oral prose learning. *Journal of Educational Psychology, 69,* 473-480.
Hosenfeld, C. (1977). A preliminary investigation of the reading strategies of successful and nonsuccessful second-language learners. *System, 5,* 110-123.
Huey, E. B. (1908). *The psychology and pedagogy of reading,* New York: Macmillan.
Johnson, P. (1982). Effects on reading comprehension of building background knowledge. *TESOL Quarterly, 16,* 503-516.
Just, M. A., & Carpenter, P. A. (1980). A theory of reading: From eye fixations to comprehension. *Psychological Review, 87,* 329-354.
Just, M. A., & Carpenter, P. A. (1984). Reading skills and skilled reading in the comprehension of text. In H. Mandl, N. L. Stein, & T. Trabasso (Eds.), *Learning and Comprehension of Text.* Hillsdale, NJ: Erlbaum Press.
Kamil, M. L., Langer, J. A., & Shanahan, T. (1985). *Understanding research in reading and writing.* Newton, MA: Allyn & Bacon.
Levin, J. R., & Lesgold, A. M. (1978). On pictures in prose. *Educational Communication and Technology, 26,* 233-243.

Lundberg, I. (1984, August). Reading Process. Paper presented at the IRA Symposium on Reading and Linguistics of the 7th World Congress of the International Association of Applied Linguistics, Brussels.

Mandl, H., Stein, N. L., & Trabasso, T. (1984). *Learning and comprehension of text*. Hillsdale, NJ: Lawrence Erlbaum Associates.

Marr, M. B. (1979). Children's comprehension of pictorial and textual event sequences. In M. L. Kamil & A. J. Moe (Eds.), *Reading research: Studies and applications*. Clemson, SC: National Reading Conference.

McCagg, P. (1984). Doctoral dissertation. Washington, DC, Georgetown University.

McDermott, R. P. (1976). *Kids make sense: An ethnographic account of the interactional management of success and failure in one first grade classroom*. Unpublished doctoral dissertation, Stanford University, Stanford, CA.

Pearson, P. D., Barr, R., Kamil M. L., & Mosenthal, P. (1984). *Handbook of reading research*. New York: Longman.

Rigg, P. (1977). The miscue-ESL project. In H. D. Brown, C. A. Yorio, & R. H. Crymes (Eds.). *On Teaching English to Speakers of Other Languages '77*, (pp. 106-118). Washington, DC: TESOL.

Samuels, S. J. (1970). Effects of pictures on learning to read, comprehension and attitudes. *Review of Educational Research, 40*, 397-407.

Steffensen, M. S. (1981). *Register, cohesion, and cross-cultural reading* (Technical Report No. 220). Urbana: University of Illinois, Center for the Study of Reading.

Thomas, J. L. (1979). The influence of pictorial illustrations with written text and previous achievement on the reading comprehension of fourth grade science students. *Journal of Research in Science Teaching, 15*, 401-405.

Tierney, R. J., & Cuningham, J. W. (1984). Research on teaching reading comprehension. In P. D. Pearson, R. Barr, M. L. Kamil, & P. Mosenthal (Eds.), *Handbook of reading research* (pp. 609-656). New York: Longman.

Footnote

[1]It should be mentioned that some researchers view ethnography and descriptive research as two distinct forms of inquiry. Kamil, Langer, and Shanahan (1985) point out that descriptive research and ethnographic research both describe, but stem from different philosophies. In descriptive studies, the investigator decides the questions to be answered and the categories in which to distribute observations prior to data collection. Ethnographic studies, on the other hand, avoid predata collection decisions. In addition descriptive studies have a quantitative outcome—even if expressed in frequencies or percentages—while ethnographic research may or may not report quantitative outcomes.

A View of Written Text as Communicative Interaction:

Implications for Reading in a Second Language

Patricia L. Carrell

Southern Illinois University

A View of Written Text as Communicative Interaction:

Implications For Reading In a Second Language

Recently, de Beaugrande (1980) and de Beaugrande and Dressler (1981) have argued that texts cannot be adequately studied by mere extension of linguistic methodology. They maintain that texts are not simply units larger than sentences, or sequences of sentences, which may be studied via purely linguistic methods. Rather, they argue that to understand texts and those properties which distinguish a text from a mere sequence of sentences, texts must be studied as they are used in communicative interaction. Drawing on basic research in cognitive science, they present cogent arguments for a communicative, interactive, procedural approach to the study of text. A central notion of their argument is that textuality—what makes a text a unified, meaningful whole, rather than merely a string of unrelated sentences— lies not in the text per se as some independent, artifactual object of study, but rather in the social and psychological activities human beings perform with it. A text is viewed as the outcome of various procedural operations, and as such, cannot be adequately described and explained in isolation from the procedures humans use to produce and receive it.[1]

If de Beaugrande and Dressler are correct, and I believe they are, then this view of written text has important implications for theories of reading (the reception of text), and in particular for theories of reading in a second language. If we agree that the second language reader must interact with the text in the comprehension process, then closer examination of the seven standards of textuality which de Beaugrande and Dressler propose for textual interaction should shed new light on the nature of that interaction in reading in a second language.

This paper examines the process of reading in a second language from the perspective of de Beaugrande and Dressler's seven standards of textuality: cohesion, coherence, intentionality, acceptability, informativity, situationality, and intertextuality. *Cohesion* is the principle that there should be connectivity among the surface elements of the text. *Coherence* is the principle that there should be connectivity among the concepts and relations underlying the text. *Intentionality* is the text producer's attitude that a cohesive, coherent text is being created for some goal. *Acceptability* is the corresponding attitude from the text receiver's perspective. *Informativity* is an index of the extent to which text occurrences are neither probable nor predictable in their context. *Situationality* is a measure of the text's relevance to a current or recoverable situation. *Intertextuality* is the principle whereby the production or comprehension of a given text depends on knowledge of and experience with other texts (other specific texts or texts in general).

This paper maintains that second language reading and reading comprehension are processes which include, among other factors, varying degrees of successful or unsuccessful interaction between the second language reader and the text in terms of these seven principles.

Second Language Reading as an Interactive Process

That reading is not a passive but rather an active, and in fact, an interactive, process between the reader and the text has been recognized for some time (Goodman, 1967, 1971; Kolers, 1969; Smith, 1971). However, it is only recently that the interactive view of reading has been acknowledged in second language reading. Early work in second language reading, specifically ESL reading, assumed a rather passive, bottom-up view of second language reading. Second language reading was viewed primarily as a decoding process: a reconstructing of the author's intended meaning via recognizing the letters and words, and building up a semantic representation of the text's meaning from the smallest textual units at the bottom to the largest at the top (Rivers, 1964, 1968; Plaister, 1968; Yorio, 1971). Problems of second language reading and reading comprehension were viewed as decoding problems. About a decade ago, the psycholinguistic model of reading began to have an impact on views of ESL reading (Goodman, 1967, 1971; Smith, 1971). ESL reading specialists such as Eskey (1970, 1973), Clarke and Silberstein (1977), Clarke (1979), Coady (1979), Mackay and Mountford (1979), and Widdowson, (1978, 1983) began to view ESL reading as an active process in which the second language reader is viewed as an active information-processor who predicts and samples only parts of the actual text. However, only since about 1979 has a truly top-down approach to second language reading been advanced (Steffensen, Joag-dev & Anderson, 1979; Carrell, 1981, 1982; Carrell & Eisterhold, 1983; Johnson, 1981, 1982; Hudson, 1982). In the top-down view of second language reading, not only is the reader an active participant in the reading process, making predictions and processing information, but everything in the reader's prior experience or background knowledge plays a potential role in the process. Lest the top-down view of second language reading be taken as a replacement for the bottom-up, decoding view, several researchers have recently emphasized that efficient and effective second language reading requires both top-down and bottom-up strategies operating interactively (Rumelhart, 1977, 1980; Sanford & Garrod, 1981; Eskey & Grabe, in press; van Dijk & Kintsch, 1983; Carrell & Eisterhold, 1983; Carrell, in press.)

If reading, which was formerly viewed as strictly passive, is an interactive process between a reader and a text, and if writing, more obviously, is also an interactive process between a writer and a text, then the whole written discourse process is a complex interaction. According to Candlin and Saedi (1983), "the discourse process of the writer . . . (is) an *elaborative* process, resulting in *text*, (and) that of the reader . . . (is) a *reductive* process, working upon the text" (p. 1). Although the discourse process may be viewed from two complementary perspectives, that of the writer and that of the reader, some of the same factors play a role in the discourse process of both the writer and the reader. These factors include the background knowledge of the writer and the reader, as well as the writer's assessment of the background knowledge of the reader, the communicative intentions of the writer, and the reader's assumptions about the communicative intentions of the writer (Candlin & Saedi, 1983, pp. 1-9). Included in background knowledge are knowledge of subject matter, genre, sociocultural and general world knowledge, and linguistic knowledge of text code. In other words, included in background knowledge are de Beaugrande and Dressler's (1981) seven components of textuality.

Interactive Second Language Reading from the Perspective of the Seven Standards of Textuality

As previously mentioned, de Beaugrande and Dressler (1981) define *text* as "a *Communicative Occurrence* which meets seven standards of *Textuality*" (p. 3). If any one of these seven standards is not satisfied, the text will not be communicative. Thus, these seven standards are taken to function as constitutive principles (in the sense of Searle, 1969, p. 33) of textual communication: They define and create the behavior. Without any one of them, the behavior which is identifiable as textual communication breaks down.

In addition to the seven constitutive standards of textuality, de Beaugrande and Dressler (1981) also discuss three regulative principles (see Searle, 1969), which control textual communication rather than define it. The three regulative principles are efficiency, effectiveness, and appropriateness.

> 1. *Efficiency* of a text, which is related to its processing ease, depends on its use in communicating with a minimum expenditure of effort by the participants.
> 2. *Effectiveness* of a text, which is related to processing depth, depends on its leaving a strong impression and creating favorable conditions for attaining a goal.
> 3. *Appropriateness* of a text is the agreement between the setting of a text and the ways in which the seven standards of textuality are upheld.

Interestingly, according to de Beaugrande and Dressler (1981, p. 34), efficiency and effectiveness tend to work against each other. On the one hand, simple language and trite content are easy to produce and receive, but may cause boredom and have little impact. In contrast, creative language and bizarre content can produce powerful effects, but may be unduly difficult to produce and receive. Hence, appropriateness mediates between these other two opposing factors to yield the proper balance between the conventional and the unconventional in each situation.

The following sections discuss each of these seven standards of textuality and the role they play in interactive reading. In general, de Beaugrande and Dressler's seven standards of textuality are conceived as being some of the specific components which constitute the construct I have previously referred to as "background knowledge" (Carrell, 1981, 1983a, 1983b, 1983c; Carrell & Eisterhold, 1983). In other words, these seven standards of textuality are a beginning at specifying in detail some of the many things which constitute background knowledge and which play a major role in interactive text processing: *top-down processing*, relating what is already known to the text being processed; and *bottom-up processing*, relating the text being processed to what is already known.

Cohesion and Coherence

Cohesion as defined by de Beaugrande and Dressler (1981) concerns the ways in which the surface elements of a text are arranged and mutually connected within a sequence. This is an extremely broad notion of cohesion, broader than Halliday and Hasan's (Halliday, 1964, p. 303; Halliday & Hasan, 1976) notion of cohesion, and includes all means of signalling surface grammatical dependencies.[2]

Coherence concerns "the ways in which the components of the textual world, that is, the configuration of concepts and relations which underlie the surface text, are mutually accessible and relevant" (de Beaugrande & Dressler, 1981, p. 4). Concepts are configurations of prior knowledge (cognitive content) in the mind, and relations are links between concepts which appear together in a textual world. Frequently, the relations are not made explicit in the text, that is, they are not mentally activated by expressions in the surface structure of the text. Rather, they are supplied mentally by the background knowledge of the producer or receiver of the text. Receivers tend to supply as many such relations as are both in their repertoire and as are needed to make sense of a text. Causality, for example, is a relation frequently left implicit: "Jack fell down and broke his crown" (de Beaugrande & Dressler, 1981, p. 5). The event of Jack's falling down is the cause of the event of Jack's breaking his crown, but this is not explicit in the text.

Although de Beaugrande and Dressler claim that cohesion and coherence are text-centered notions (designating operations directed at the text materials), in the concept of coherence it is clear that they have moved beyond the text per se. Coherence is clearly not a feature of a text as an artifact, but rather as the outcome of cognitive processes by text users. A text does not cohere by itself, but rather via the interaction between text-presented knowledge and the text user's stored knowledge.

The role of cohesion and coherence, and in particular the relationship between cohesion and coherence, has recently become a focus of attention and research in second language text production and reception. The following discussion of these two standards of textuality is, for the most part, limited to text reception (i.e., second language reading), but some of the research mentioned applies equally to second language writing.

Chapman (1979) found that native English-speaking children in Britain who were reading fluently were able to complete anaphoric relations in a cloze test, and he concluded that mastery of such textual features, including cohesive ties, is a central factor in fluent reading and reading comprehension. According to Cohen, Glasman, Rosenbaum-Cohen, Ferrara, and Fine (1979), foreign readers of English texts in the sciences and economics often do not pick up on conjunctive words in their specialized texts. They argue that nonnative speakers read more locally than native speakers and, because they do not attend to conjunctive ties, they have trouble synthesizing information across sentences and paragraphs. Williams (1983) has also discussed the importance of recognizing cohesive ties in reading in a foreign language, and has suggested teaching materials and methods to remedy ESL readers' deficiencies. He proposes a system of symbols and strategies for teaching foreign readers how to use cohesive signals in order to increase their comprehension of texts.

Connor (1984a) has studied both cohesion and coherence in advanced ESL learners' writing and discovered that although advanced ESL writers use about the same proportion of cohesive devices as native writers, they lack the variety of native writers. This is especially true in the category of lexical cohesion, where ESL writers tend to overuse repetition, and underuse synonyms and collocation. Connor attributes this to general deficiencies in ESL learners' vocabularies and comments that this appears to be related to similar results with good and poor native English readers (Witte & Faigley, 1981). However, she suggests that in order to be most illuminating, cohesion must be studied in conjunction with coherence.

Without denying the importance of cohesion and the role it plays in efficient reading and reading comprehension, the relationship between cohesion and coherence remains a knotty problem. A number of researchers have taken exception to Halliday and Hasan's (1976) basic premise that coherence is created by cohesion—a premise we might label as the strong view of the relationship. Morgan and Sellner (1980), Steffensen (1981), Tierney and Mosenthal (1981), and Carrell (1982, 1983a, 1984a, 1985b) have all argued that such a view of cohesion is an attempt to locate coherence in the text and ignores the contribution of the reader in constructing textual meaning. According to these researchers, it is textual coherence which effects cohesion, not the reverse. Cohesion is the result of a coherent rendering of content. Thus, these researchers reject the strong statement of cohesion, that it creates coherence, but they appear to accept a weaker position, that cohesion is related to coherence.

Further empirical research by Steffensen (in press) questions even the weak view of the relationship between cohesion and coherence. This research was based on the expectation that while cohesion may not create coherence, it ought to be positively related to coherence. Thus, a text written on a culturally familiar topic, that is, a more coherent text reflecting greater understanding of the events involved, was expected to have a proportionally greater number of cohesive ties than a text written on a culturally unfamiliar topic. This premise was not supported. Texts produced as recall protocols by both native English speakers (Americans) and nonnative English speakers (Indians) on both familiar and unfamiliar topics showed no differences in the number of reference, repetition, ellipsis, substitution, and conjunctive cohesive ties. Steffensen's results show that cohesive devices are used with as great a frequency in texts which are incoherent and/or culturally distorted, as with texts which are coherent and/or culturally undistorted. Thus, Steffensen's research shows no support for the strong claim that cohesion creates coherence, nor for the weak claim that it is correlated with coherence. Steffensen concludes that "a bit of caution is called for in using cohesion as a methodology for overcoming problems involved in reading in a foreign language" (in press). Steffensen's research suggests that the two standards of cohesion and coherence may be independent of each other. Mastering cohesive devices is part of achieving competence in a second language and, therefore, should not be ignored in the classroom. Nonetheless, we must also pay attention to other factors which influence reading and reading comprehension, including background knowledge which plays such a large role in coherence and other standards of textuality.

Cohesion and coherence are the two most basic standards of textuality. They indicate how the component elements of the text fit together and make sense. However, as de Beaugrande and Dressler (1981) point out, cohesion and coherence alone cannot provide the absolute distinction between texts and nontexts. People can and do make use of texts which, for various reasons, do not seem fully cohesive and coherent. Therefore, there must be other factors contributing to textuality—factors which make it possible for text producers and receivers to uphold cohesion and coherence in texts for which it would otherwise be difficult or impossible.

Intentionality and Acceptability

Intentionality and acceptability, respectively, concern the producer's and the receiver's attitudes that a set of language occurrences should constitute a cohesive and coherent text fulfilling the producer's intentions and being useful or relevant to the receiver. As text users, we fulfill the standards of intentionality and acceptability by intending each language occurrence to be a cohesive, coherent text relevant to human plans and goals and by expecting the recipient to accept the text in that way. Producers' and receivers' attitudes and assumptions play a large role in determining whether a potential text is a text. Producers and receivers must intend and accept the language configuration in question as a cohesive and coherent text. If they do not, the object is not a text.

De Beaugrande and Dressler (1981) discuss these two standards in terms of Grice's cooperative principle and its attendant maxims. With clever demonstration texts they illustrate how texts which require the receiver to make important inferences are often more effective than versions which make everything explicit. (One familiar example they cite, from the telephone company: "Call us before you dig. You may not be able to afterwards.") Receivers support coherence and cohesion, and tolerate potential disturbances in cohesion and coherence by making their own contributions to the sense of the text. Thus, the principles of intentionality and acceptability play a role in the unambiguous use and perception of potentially ambiguous utterances. Conversely, text may break down when intentionality and acceptability are not upheld. For example, an uncooperative text participant may deliberately block communication by refusing acceptance, for example, by not recovering or upholding coherence.

From the perspective of second language reading, if text producers and receivers do not share common knowledge and assumptions, they may not be able to uphold coherence. The native author may intend cohesion and coherence, but the nonnative reader may be unable to accept the writer's intention. Carrell and Eisterhold (1983) report an example wherein cultural/religious values made it impossible for a devout Muslim ESL student to accept a passage about prejudice in religion.[3]

Informativity

The fifth standard of textuality is informativity, which concerns the extent to which the content and/or form of the text is contextually expected and predictable. The higher the degree of contextual probability, the lower the level of informativity: First-order informativity consists of the trivial and predictable; second-order informativity consists of probable options and is the normal standard for textual communication; and third-order informativity consists of the improbable, odd, or totally unexpected. In achieving the appropriate level of informativity, a delicate balance must be maintained between efficiency (ease of processing) and effectiveness (interest). A text with higher degrees of informativity increases processing demands, but is usually more interesting; a text with lower informativity is easier to process, but may be less interesting, even boring.

Usually the concept of informativity is applied to content only, and in communicative language teaching is referred to as the "information gap" which exists between the text and the reader. However, de Beaugrande and Dressler (1981) show that informativity may apply equally to form as well as content. Texts may have conventional cohesion (form) and unconventional, high informativity in coherence (content): "All our yesterdays have lighted fools the way to dusty death" (Shakespeare, *Macbeth*). Conversely, texts may have conventional coherence (content) and unconventional, high informativity in cohesion (form): "Him who disobeys, me disobeys" (Milton, *Paradise Lost*).

The delicate balance between efficiency and effectiveness may be achieved via the flow of expectations from one text segment to subsequent text segments; subsequent text segments may upgrade or downgrade the informativity of preceding text segments. The following example is from de Beaugrande and Dressler:

> Twenty-year-old Willie B. is a diehard TV addict. He hates news and talk shows, but he loves football and gets so excited over food commercials that he sometimes charges at the set, waving a fist. Says a friend: 'He's like a little child.'
>
> Willie B. is a 450-lb gorilla at the Atlanta Zoo. In December a Tennessee TV dealer heard about Willie B.'s lonely life as the zoo's only gorilla and gave him a TV set. (1981, p. 151)

The first paragraph leads the receiver to assume the text is about a human being; encountering the first sentence in the second paragraph, *Willie B. is a 450-lb gorilla at the Atlanta Zoo,* creates an immediate third-order informativity effect, followed by backward downgrading. The receiver regresses and finds that the preceding material deals only with typical, not determinate knowledge about humans. Forward downgrading is provided by the last sentence: The atypical situation and actions of the gorilla are revealed as caused and enabled by a human agent. The second paragraph might easily have been placed before the first one, but the effectiveness of the text would have been much lower. By ordering the paragraphs in this manner, the producer of this text has made use of receivers' expectations to markedly increase the impact of the text.

The delicate balance between efficiency and effectiveness in informativity suggests that we reexamine the notion of readability as it applies to second language reading. If readability is defined as the extent to which a text is suitable for reception by given groups, we cannot optimize readability simply by striving for the best possible match between text-presented knowledge and prior world knowledge. The resulting text would possess too low a degree of informativity and, therefore, be devoid of interest. "Readability must *not* be defined as the expenditure of the least effort (despite Hirsch, 1977), but rather as the appropriate proportion between required effort and resulting insights" (de Beaugrande & Dressler, 1981, p. 213).

Situationality

Situationality, the sixth standard of textuality, concerns the relevance of a text to its situational setting. This standard concerns the reasonableness of the inferences text users make depending on their knowledge of assumptions about the situation in which the text occurs. For example, the situation in which a road sign such as "Slow - Children at Play" occurs affects the reasonableness of the interpretation of *slow* as a request to motorists to reduce speed as opposed to an announcement of the mental or physical capacities of the children. Thus, along with the standards of intentionality and acceptability, situationality plays a role in the unambiguous use and perception of potentially ambiguous utterances.

Situation may also drastically affect the means of cohesion used in a text. The situation of a road sign governs its cryptic, inexplicit form as opposed to a longer, more explicitly cohesive version; speeding motorists would not have time to process a more explicitly cohesive version.

However, the effects of situation on text are very rarely unmediated. That is, the effect of situation is rarely completely objective. Text participants feed their own beliefs and goals, and their prior knowledge and expectations about how the real world operates into their models of the communicative situation. It is these models of the situation which affect text. To the extent that nonnative readers' models of the communicative situation differ from native readers'/authors' models, this will affect text reception. Nonnative readers' models of various situations may affect the way certain linguistic speech acts within those situations are perceived. For example, requests may be perceived as suggestions, suggestions as requests, invitations as inquiries, and so on.

Furthermore, as de Beaugrande and Dressler (1981) point out, situation models are often not static, merely to be monitored in text use. Situation is often dynamic, being managed and affected by text use. That is, one prime function of text is to guide and manage a situation in a manner favorable to the text producer's goals. In fact, successful text users frequently disguise their situation-managings as situation-monitorings, creating the impression that things are going the desired way in the normal course of events.

Since many goals are not attainable through the actions of one agent, situation management may entail negotiation of goals. Thus, texts (both oral and written) become means of cooperative goal negotiation and are correlated with discourse actions and applied to a situation. As de Beaugrande and Dressler state:

> The correlations involved are far from simple reflections of the apperceivable evidence in the situation alone. Instead, the con-

tent of texts is usually removed via mediation from the evidence, according to the producer's outlook, beliefs, plans, and goals. Whether a text is acceptable may depend not on the 'correctness' of its 'reference' to the 'real world,' but rather on its believability and relevance to the participants' outlook regarding the situation. (1981, p. 179)

Intertextuality

Intertextuality, the seventh and final standard, subsumes a number of factors which make the production and reception of a given text dependent upon the participant's knowledge of other texts. For example, a road sign which reads "Resume Speed" can only make sense in the context of a previous text which requested motorists to reduce speed. The text "Every litter bit hurts" will have an added dimension of meaning to one who knows the related text "Every little bit helps." The effectiveness of many literary texts depends upon implicit text allusion to other, often well-known texts.

In addition to knowledge of and prior experience with other specific texts, intertextuality includes the effects of prior knowledge of and experience with texts in general, and with different text types or genres. Recent empirical research has shown the powerful effects on both first and second language reading of formal schemata or background knowledge of rhetorical organization and rhetorical conventions (Meyer, 1975; Mandler, 1978; Carrell, 1984c, 1985a; Hinds, 1983a, 1983b; Connor, 1984b, Connor & McCagg, 1983a, 1983b). Prior knowledge of typical or conventional English text types (literary, poetic, scientific, descriptive, narrative, argumentative, problem/solution, comparison, etc.) has been shown to affect second language reading. Thus, the important role of this standard of textuality—intertextuality—in an interactive model of second language reading has already been empirically demonstrated.

Conclusion

This brief review of de Beaugrande and Dressler's seven principles of textuality has been able only to skim the surface of the potential role they play in second language reading. Although limited, its purpose has been to show the relevance of each of the seven principles to second language reading. I would maintain that any interactive approach to second language reading, especially one which incorporates a strong top-down perspective, will have to include notions such as intentionality, acceptability, informativity, situationality, and intertextuality, as well as cohesion and coherence. The ultimate taxonomy in which these, as well as other, notions occur remains an open question.

In order to better understand the complexities of second language reading, what is needed now is more theoretical and empirical research on the specific role played by each of these seven standards of textuality, both individually as well as collectively, in interactive second language reading.

References

de Beaugrande, R. (1980). *Text, discourse, and process*. Norwood, NJ: Ablex.
de Beaugrande, R., & Dressler, W. (1981). *Introduction to text linguistics*. London: Longman.
Candlin, C. N., & Saedi, K. L. (1983). Processes of discourse. *Journal of Applied Language Study, 1,* 1-51.
Carrell, P. L. (1981). Culture-specific schemata in L2 comprehension. In R. A. Orem & J. F. Haskell (Eds.), *Selected papers from the ninth Illinois TESOL/BE annual convention, the first midwest TESOL conference,* (pp. 123-132). Chicago: Illinois TESOL/BE.
Carrell, P. L. (1982). Cohesion is not coherence. *TESOL Quarterly, 16,* 479-488.
Carrell, P. L. (1983a). [Reply to Ghadessy]. *TESOL Quarterly, 17,* 687-691.
Carrell, P. L. (1983b). Background knowledge in second language comprehension. *Language Learning and Communication, 2,* 25-34.
Carrell, P. L. (1983c). Some issues in studying the role of schemata, or background knowledge, in second language comprehension. *Reading in a Foreign Language, 1,* 81-92.
Carrell, P. L. (1983d). Three components of background knowledge in reading comprehension. *Language Learning, 33,* 183-207.
Carrell, P. L. (1984a). [Reply to Rankin]. *TESOL Quarterly, 18,* 161-168.
Carrell, P. L. (1984b). Evidence of a formal schema in second language comprehension. *Language Learning, 34,* 87-112.
Carrell, P. L. (1984c). The effects of rhetorical organization on ESL readers. *TESOL Quarterly, 18,* 441-469.
Carrell, P. L. (1985a). Facilitating ESL reading by teaching text structure. *TESOL Quarterly, 19,* 727-752.
Carrell, P. L. (1985b). [Reply to Ghadessy]. *TESOL Quarterly, 19,* 382-390.
Carrell P. L. (in press). Some causes of text-boundedness and schema interference. In P. L. Carrell, J. Devine, & D. Eskey (Eds.), *Interactive approaches to second language reading*. New York: Cambridge University Press.
Carrell, P. L., & Eisterhold, J. C. (1983). Schema theory and ESL reading pedagogy. *TESOL Quarterly, 17,* 553-573.
Chapman, L. J. (1979). Confirming children's use of cohesive ties in text: Pronouns. *The Reading Teacher, 33,* 317-322.
Clarke, M. A. (1979). Reading in Spanish and English: Evidence from adult ESL students. *Language Learning, 29,* 121-150.
Clarke, M. A., & Silberstein, S. (1977). Toward a realization of psycholinguistic principles in the ESL reading class. *Language Learning, 27,* 135-154.
Coady, J. (1979). A psycholinguistic model of the ESL reader. In R. Maclay, B. Barkman, & R. R. Jordan (Eds.) *Reading in a second language,* (pp. 5-12). Rowley, MA: Newbury House.
Cohen, A., Glasman, H., Rosenbaum-Cohen, P. R., Ferrara, J., & Fine, J. (1979). Reading English for specialized purposes: Discourse analysis and the use of student informants. *TESOL Quarterly, 13,* 551-564.
Connor, U. (1984a). A study of cohesion and coherence in English as a second language students' writing. *Papers in Linguistics, 17,* 301-316.

Connor, U. (1984b). Recall of text: Differences between first and second language readers. *TESOL Quarterly, 18,* 239-256.
Connor, U., & McCagg. P. (1983a). Cross-cultural differences and perceived quality in written paraphrases of English expository prose. *Applied Linguistics, 4,* 259-268
Connor U., & McCagg, P. (1983b). *Text structure and ESL learners' reading comprehension.* Unpublished manuscript.
Eskey, D. (1970). A new technique for the teaching of reading to advanced students. *TESOL Quarterly, 4,* 315-322.
Eskey, D. (1973). A model program for teaching advanced reading to students of English as a second language. *Language Learning, 23,* 169-184.
Eskey, D., & Grabe, W. (in press). General implications of an interactive model for ESL reading instruction. In P. L. Carrell, J. Devine & D. Eskey (Eds.), *Interactive approaches to second language reading.* New York: Cambridge University Press.
Goodman, K. S. (1967). Reading: A psycholinguistic guessing game. *Journal of the Reading Specialist, 6,* 126-135.
Goodman, K. S. (1971). Psycholinguistic universals in the reading process. In P. Pinsleur & T. Quinn (Eds.), *The psychology of second language learning* (pp. 135-142). Cambridge: Cambridge University.
Halliday, M. A. K. (1964). The linguistic study of literary texts. In H. Hunt (Ed.), *Proceedings of the ninth international congress of linguistics* (pp. 302-307). The Hague: Mouton.
Halliday, M. A. K., & Hasan, R. (1976). *Cohesion in English.* London: Longman.
Hinds, J. (1983, March). Retention of information using a Japanese style of presentation. Paper presented at the 17th Annual TESOL Convention, Toronto.
Hinds, J. (1983b). Contrastive rhetoric: Japanese and English. *ext, 3,* 183-195.
Hirsch, E. D. (1977). *The philosophy of composition.* Chicago: University of Chicago.
Hudson, T. (1982). The effects of induced schemata on the "short circuit" in L2 reading: Non-decoding factors in L2 reading performance. *Language Learning, 32,* 1-31.
Johnson, P. (1981). Effects on reading comprehension of language complexity and cultural background of a text. *TESOL Quarterly, 15,* 169-181.
Johnson, P. (1982). Effects on reading comprehension of building background knowledge. *TESOL Quarterly, 16,* 503-516.
Kolers, P. A. (1969). Reading is only incidentally visual. In K. S. Goodman & J. T. Fleming (Eds.), *Psycholinguistics and the teaching of reading* (pp. 8-16). Newark, DE: International Reading Association.
Mackay, R., & Mountford, A. (1979). Reading for information. In R. Mackay, B. Barkman, & R. R. Jordan (Eds.), *Reading in a second language* (pp. 106-141). Rowley, MA: Newbury House.
Mandler, J. M. (1978). A code in the node: The use of a story schema in retrieval. *Discourse Processes, 1,* 14-35.
Meyer, B. J. F. (1975). *The organization of prose and its effects on memory.* Amsterdam: North-Holland.
Morgan, J. L., & Sellner, M. B. (1980). Discourse and linguistic theory. In R. J. Spiro, B. C. Bruce, & W. F. Brewer (Eds.), *Theoretical issues in reading comprehension* (pp. 165-200). Hillsdale, NJ: Lawrence Erlbaum.
Plaister, T. (1968). Reading instruction for college level foreign students. *TESOL Quarterly, 2,* 164-168.
Rivers, W. (1964). *The psychologist and the foreign-language teacher.* Chicago: University of Chicago.
Rivers, W. (1968). *Teaching foreign language skills.* Chicago: University of Chicago.

Rumelhart, D. E. (1977). Understanding and summarizing brief stories. In D. LaBerge & S. J. Samuels (Eds.), *Basic processes in reading: perception and comprehension* (pp. 265-303). Hillsdale, NJ: Lawrence Erlbaum.
Rumelhart, D. E. (1980). Schemata: The building blocks of cognition. In R. J. Spiro, B. C. Bruce, & W. F. Brewer (Eds.), *Theoretical issues in reading comprehension* (pp. 33-58). Hillsdale, NJ: Lawrence Erlbaum.
Sanford, A. J., & Garrod, S. C. (1981). *Understanding written language*. New York: John Wiley & Sons.
Searle, J. R. (1969). *Speech acts*. London: Cambridge University.
Smith, F. (1971). *Understanding reading: A psycholinguistic analysis of reading and learning to read*. New York: Holt, Rinehart and Winston.
Steffensen, M. S. (1981). *Register, cohesion, and cross-cultural reading* (Technical Report No. 220). Urbana: University of Illinois, Center for the Study of Reading.
Steffensen, M. S. (in press). Changes in cohesion in the recall of native and foreign texts. In P. L. Carrell, J. Devine, & D. Eskey (Eds.), *Interactive approaches to second language reading*. New York: Cambridge University.
Steffensen, M. S., Joag-dev, C. & Anderson, R. C. (1979). A cross-cultural perspective on reading comprehension. *Reading Research Quarterly, 15*, 10-29.
Tierney, R. J., & Mosenthal, J. (1981). *The cohesion concept's relationship to the coherence of text* (Technical Report No. 221). Urbana: University of Illinois, Center for the Study of Reading.
van Dijk, T. A., & Kintsch, W. (1983). *Strategies of discourse comprehension*. New York: Academic Press.
Widdowson, H. G. (1978). *Teaching language as communication*. London: Oxford University.
Widdowson, H. G. (1983). *Learning purpose and language use*. London: Oxford University.
Williams, R. (1983). Teaching the recognition of cohesive ties in reading a foreign language. *Reading in a Foreign Language, 1*, 35-53.
Witte, S. P., & Faigley, L. (1981). Coherence, cohesion, and writing quality. *College Composition and Communication, 22*, 189-204.
Woods, W. (1970). Transition network grammars for natural language analysis. *Communications of the Association for Computing Machinery, 13*, 591-606.
Yorio, C. A. (1971). Some sources of reading problems for foreign language learners. *Language Learning, 21*, 107-115.

Author's Notes

Without implying that they agree with everything I say, or that I was wise enough to have accepted all their comments, I wish to thank Andrew D. Cohen and Margaret Steffensen for reading and commenting on this paper.

Footnotes

[1] In fact, cross-cultural research suggests that what "counts" as a text varies from one culture to another, further supporting this inseparability notion of de Beaugrande and Dressler (1981). For example, Steffensen (personal communication, 1985) has examples of texts from Australian aborigines which are not considered texts for Americans, due to differences in textual organization. The oral narrative story schema for

these aborigine texts follow a type of "ancestral" narrative which Americans feel is incoherent as a text.

²In fact, de Beaugrande and Dressler (1981) envisage a type of on-line, real-time, performance grammar, such as an augmented transition network (Woods, 1970), rather than a competence grammar. "In a transition network, the structures of phrases and clauses are operationalized as means to build and test hypotheses about the types of elements to use or expect at any given time. Hence, these networks capture the grammatical *strategies* and *expectations* of language users; and they express the rules of grammar as *procedures* [italics added] for using the rules." (de Beaugrande and Dressler, 1981, p. 50).

³Footnote 1, about cross-cultural research and what is considered a text, is relevant here, also.

Comments on Carrell

Sandra Silberstein

University of Washington

Carrell's paper brings to mind a comment made by the linguist Linde (personal communication, 1984) in another research context: "All of us seem to be backing into the same mystery." In this case, the mystery comprises the interactions within texts, and between reader and text, which produce textuality. Carrell's paper underscores the conceptual importance of such interactions for ESL reading theory.

In this regard, ESL theorists share an evolving perspective with scholars from diverse disciplines. My goal here is to demonstrate the utility of a cross-disciplinary approach to textual theories. As an example, we find complementary approaches to themes raised by Carrell being developed in literary and film theory. Currently, at least three strains of textual criticism in the humanities focus on the interaction of reader and text: reader response theory, social theory, and feminist film criticism.

The first of these, reader response theory, illustrates the most obvious connection to our work. This approach developed as a challenge to the traditional notion of literary text as autonomous aesthetic object. Critics, such as Fetterly (1978), Fish (1980), and Iser (1978), argue that meaning is not autonomous, but develops in the context of interaction between reader and text. The location of meaning in reader response, with corresponding de-emphasis of authorial intent, resonates with current ESL reading theory. Of particular interest for the reading theorist are the detailed theoretical discussions of both reader and text.

Social (particularly Marxist literary) theory explores the relation between text and ideology. Ideology here refers to a shared picture of the world. Marxist literary theorists inquire how a culture reproduces itself through the (re)creation of meaning in texts. Prominent among these critics are Williams (1973, 1976, 1977), Eagleton (1983, 1984), and Jamison (1971, 1972). The generation of meaning occurs through an interaction of text within context, among reader, and text and context. This approach provides useful parallels to de Beaugrande and Dressler's (1981) intertextuality. Central to Marxist literary theory is the notion that textual meaning is created through the relation of a text to other texts and to the prevailing ideology. This location of context in ideology might profitably inform ESL reading theory. Context thereby becomes a shared set of values; context is value-laden for the reader. So considered, the relation of text to context is reflective. Texts serve to (re) create our cultural context.

Perhaps the most productive theory of textuality comes from feminist film theory. In *Alice Doesn't*, de Lauretis (1984) uses Marxist, psychoanalytic, and semiological theory (the theory of signs) to explain the creation of gender in the text of modern film. Once again, we see the interaction of text and receiver, in this case the interaction of a gendered viewer with a semiologically familiar film in order to make the image of the generic woman the text on which the film is written. De Lauretis' union of competing intellectual traditions will make her important to future discussions of textuality. Her interrogation of the subjective consciousness by which an individual interacts with a text provides a useful model for reading theory.

This brief overview can only suggest the productive interactions possible in cross-disciplinary work. These possibilities should encourage second languge researchers to interact with the texts from other disciplines in order to build a truly comprehensive theory of textuality.

References

de Beaugrande, R., & Dressler, W. (1981) *Introduction to text linguistics*. London: Longman.
de Lauretis, T. (1984). *Alice doesn't: Feminism, semiotics, cinema*. Bloomington: Indiana University.
Eagleton, T. (1983). *Literary theory: An introduction*. Minneapolis: University of Minnesota.
Eagleton, T. (1984). *The function of criticism*. London: Verso.
Fetterly, J. (1978). *The resisting reader*. Bloomington: Indiana University.

Fish, S. (1980). *Is there text in this class?* Cambridge, MA: Harvard University.
Iser, W. (1978). *The act of reading.* Baltimore: Johns Hopkins University.
Jamison, F. (1971). *Marxism and form.* Princeton, NJ: Princeton University.
Jamison, F. (1972). *The prison-house of language.* Princeton, NJ: Princeton University.
Williams, R. (1973). *The country and the city.* Oxford: Oxford University.
Williams, R (1976). *Keywords: A vocabulary of culture and society.* London: Fontana/ Croom Helm.
Williams, R. (1977). *Marxism and literature.* Oxford: Oxford University.

Additional Suggested Readings

Reader Response Theory

Bleich, D. (1975). *Readings and feelings: An introduction to subjective criticism.* Urbana, IL: National Council of Teachers of English.
Bleich, D. (1978). *Subjective criticism.* Baltimore: Johns Hopkins Press.
Fetterly, J. (1978). *The resisting reader.* Bloomington: Indiana University.
Fish, S. (1980). *Is there a text in this class?* Cambridge, MA: Harvard University Press.
Iser, W. (1978). *The act of reading.* Baltimore: Johns Hopkins University Press.
Mailloux, S. (1982). *Interpretive conventions.* Ithaca, NY: Cornell University Press.
Rosenblatt, L. (1978). *The reader, the text, the poem.* Carbondale: Southern Illinois University Press.
Suleiman, S., & Crossman, I. (Eds.). (1980). *The reader and the text.* Princeton, NJ: Princeton University Press.
Thompkins, J. (1980). *Reader-response criticism.* Baltimore: Johns Hopkins University Press.

Marxist Literary Theory

Althusser, L. (1977). *Lenin and philosophy and other essays* (B. Brewster, Trans.). London: New Left Books. (Original work published 1966).
Belsey, C. (1980). *Critical practice.* New York: Methuen.
Bennett, T. (1979). *Formalism and marxism.* New York: Methuen.
Berger, J. (1972). *Ways of seeing.* New York: Penguin.
Eagleton, T. (1983). *Literary theory: An introduction.* Minneapolis: University of Minnesota Press.
Eagleton, T. (1984). *The function of criticism.* London: Verso.
Hawkes, T. (1977). *Structuralism and semiotics.* Berkeley: University of California.
Jamison, F. (1971). *Marxism and form.* Princeton, NJ: Princeton University Press.
Jamison, F. (1972). *The prison-house of language.* Princeton, NJ: Princeton University Press.
Macherey, P. (1978). *Toward a theory of literary production.* (G. Wall, Trans.). London: Routledge and Kegan Paul. (Original work published in 1966).
Riley, M. (1982). *Marxism and deconstruction.* Baltimore: Johns Hopkins University Press.
Volosinov, V. N. (1973). *Marxism and the philosophy of language.* (L. Matejka and I. R. Titunik, Trans.). New York: Seminar Press. (Original work published 1930).
Williams, R. (1973). *The country and the city.* Oxford: Oxford University Press.
Williams, R. (1976). *Keywords: A vocabulary of culture and society.* London: Fontana/ Croom Helm.

Williams, R. (1977). *Marxism and literature*. Oxford: Oxford University Press.

Feminist Film Theory

de Lauretis, T. (1984). *Alice doesn't: Feminism, semiotics, cinema*. Bloomington: Indiana University Press.
Gledhill, C. (1978). Recent developments in feminist criticism. *Quarterly Review of Film Studies, 3*, 457-93.
Johnston, C. (Ed.). (1974). *Notes on women's cinema*. London: Society for Education in Film and Television.
Kaplan, E. A. (1983). *Women and film: Both sides of the camera*. New York: Methuen.
Kay, K., & Peary, G. (Eds.). (1977). *Women and cinema: A critical anthology*. New York: Dutton.
Kuhn, A. (1982). *Women's pictures*. London: Routledge & Kegan Paul.
Lesage, J. (1974). Feminist film criticism: Theory and practice. *Women and film, 5/6*, 12-14.
Lesage, J. (1976). *Feminism and film: Critical approaches. Camera Obscura, 1 (Fall)*, 3-10.
Mulvey, L. (1975). Visual pleasure and narrative cinema. *Screen, 16* (3).
Silverman, K. (1983). *The subject of semiotics*. New York: Oxford University Press.

The Effect of Context and Culture
On Children's L2 Reading: A Review

Margaret S. Steffensen

Illinois State University

The Effect of Context and Culture on Children's L2 Reading: A Review

Since the late 1970s, a number of studies have investigated the effect of cultural background knowledge upon the comprehension, memory, and recall of texts. In the case of adults, it has been shown that when a reader and writer share cultural assumptions and knowledge about social systems and rituals, there is a much higher level of interaction of the reader with the text than occurs when such assumptions and knowledge are not shared (Steffensen, Joag-dev, & Anderson, 1979; Steffensen & Colker, 1982; Carrell, 1981). Many of these studies involved a written procedure in which subjects were instructed to recall the entire text in wording as close to the original as possible (see, for example, Steffensen et al., 1979). However, using an adaptation of the Fillmore-Kaye procedure (Fillmore, 1981) in which a subject moves through a text one clause at a time, explaining what has been read and understood up to that point and making predictions about what follows, reveals a much more highly elaborated system of inferencing than is possible to discern when subjects are restricted to verbatim recall (Steffensen, 1986).

It can also be shown that the same processing occurs in an oral modality. If subjects are asked to recall oral texts that are based on their own culture and the dominant culture in which theirs is encapsulated (Freedle & Hall, 1975), the same pattern of elaborations of the native text and distortions of the foreign text are found as when the texts are read. This phenomenon can have significant effects on the delivery of a variety of social services since it has been incorrectly assumed that if someone can understand and speak a language, any nontechnical message in that language will also be understood.

Given the wide range of effects that cultural background knowledge has, it is quite remarkable that so little attention has been directed to the same phenomenon in children, particularly given the numbers of ESL students in American classrooms. This can be attributed to a number of causes. First, the methodology most commonly used, reading with a complete oral recall, lends itself best to working with adults, especially when it is a second language for the subject. However, preliminary research by Steffensen indicates that the Fillmore-Kaye procedure is effective with children and can provide the insights needed to assess the impact upon top-down processes of the match between the reader's cultural context and that undergirding the text.

Second, there is some evidence that children do not have highly articulated cultural schemata (Goodman & Goodman, 1978). Such a position would attribute only minimum interference to reading a text based on a foreign culture. Thus, reading a story about a birthday party in the US would be no more difficult for a child from another culture than reading a neutral text about the habits of the bald eagle. There would not be a highly developed schema about birthday celebrations in the native culture that would interfere with the processing of information in the target text.

Third, a reluctance to use children as subjects may be the result of the emphasis on teaching at the graphemic or decoding level, rather than at the level of comprehension. While a great deal of lip service is being paid to teaching comprehension, many practitioners still believe their first responsibility is decoding, with comprehension following more or less automatically as a result of that behavior. Furthermore, many teacher trainers conceptualize reading instruction as a hierarchy of skills with the foundation being control of the graphemic system. These attitudes and beliefs are further reinforced by the materials that are available for classroom use. In an analysis of hundreds of hours of classroom instruction, Durkin (1978) found only a small proportion devoted to comprehension. A focus on decoding would tend to direct research on beginning reading away from higher-level processes and the effect of the larger context, since they would not be seen as particularly relevant at that point of development. Related to this is the fact that many adults think of children's reading as a classroom activity divorced from the child's life outside the school. In this view, basal readers do not provide real communication events about real life but are for practice and skill building. It is not seen as necessary or even possible for beginning readers to bring their world knowledge to bear on texts that are so devoid of content that comprehension is not even an issue to be considered.

Finally, by working with proficient adult readers who have mastered decoding skills and who respond to syntactic/contextual constraints in their native language, there is more certainty that the interference found does involve higher-level processes, such as the absence of content schemata, rather than these lower-level skills. With children, there might be some tendency to attribute the results to lack of skills, rather than to lack of background information. Furthermore, possessing a higher level of metacomprehension skills, adults would be more skilled in monitoring and communicating about their ongoing reading processes.

The methodology used in this study of cross-cultural reading comprehension is not regarded as equally suitable for children and adults. Some researchers may be working under the assumption that children have so little cultural knowledge that it cannot be an important factor in reading comprehension, especially when the pedagogical focus is on decoding and in-class reading. However, there have been studies focused on top-down processes as well as a few that consider specifically the impact of cultural discrepancies upon the behavior of the young readers.

Studies of the Impact of Context on Children's Reading

There is a considerable body of evidence on the importance of context for the comprehension of children's reading of both native language and foreign language materials. A large number of research studies were derived from Goodman's (1967) description of reading as an active process in which the reader forms expectations about the material being read, then samples the text to confirm or revise the predictions. In this view, there is an interaction between the reader's store of information and the ability to make linguistic predictions, which influences what the reader expects to find during the processing of text. Furthermore, a text must be a semantic whole for the most effective use of previous knowledge in the comprehension of additional information from the text.

Working within Goodman's framework, Clarke and Silberstein (1977) mention semantic relevance as a consideration, along with level of linguistic difficulty, in the selection of reading materials for L2 readers. Students with the necessary schematic knowledge are more likely to be able to handle a linguistically difficult passage than those without this knowledge. While there is an emphasis on such traditional methods of L2 instruction as developing vocabulary and control of syntax in the lesson plans that they propose, there is also attention to processing at the level of discourse which reflects their concern with comprehension.

The importance of both the linguistic and the semantic context are found in studies which analyzed the miscues produced during oral reading (Goodman, 1965). Lopez (1977) examined the oral reading behavior in Spanish of Hispanic children. She found a difference in the miscues produced in reading words in lists and words in text: Significant numbers of words that were mispronounced in reading lists were read correctly when they appeared in a text. Furthermore, when words were misread in the text, the miscues tended to preserve meaning. These findings support the claim that background knowledge can have a facilitating effect on text comprehension. De Silva (1983) also studied the oral reading of Mexican-American children and found support for the claim that background of experience enters into the process. Barrera (1983) stresses the importance of reading aloud to Spanish-speaking children because that increases their conceptual knowledge and aids in developing reading competence.

Eaton (1983), in a study of field dependence and field independence in Spanish speakers, found more meaning preserving miscues in Spanish than in English, suggesting that the level at which text processing occurs is affected by the code of the text. Another study analyzed first and second language errors of 7th graders reading French texts (Cziko, 1980). The question Cziko addressed was whether second language learners, because they were less familiar with the vocabulary than native speakers were, used top-down strategies to facilitate text comprehension. In fact, the evidence is that second language readers pay more attention to graphic information than do first language readers. In this study, subjects were asked to read a text aloud for understanding. Native speakers made more deletion and insertion errors, while intermediate students of French made more errors involving the substitution of visually similiar words. Cziko concluded that intermediate students were more sensitive to graphic than contextual information, while the reverse situation held for native speakers. The strategies readers use, therefore, appear to be related to their level of reading competence. This supports an earlier finding (Cziko, 1978) that native speakers and advanced French as a second language students were aided by discourse constraints while intermediate students were not. He concluded that "the perception of a text as an integrated whole may in itself be an aid to comprehension for the fluent reader" (1978, p. 48).

The importance of top-down processes was advanced by Hewitt (1980) after a study of L1 remedial reading instruction of 12- and 13-year-olds. He found that low-level processes traditionally associated with reading problems (decoding and understanding of vocabulary and syntactic structures) had less explanatory power than higher-level processes involving limited schemata and inappropriate interaction of readers' schemata and text. Hosenfeld (1984) describes a strategy for improving foreign language reading which focuses attention on the linguistic context and use of world knowledge. Students in remediation were guided away from their ineffective reliance on glossaries by the strategy of substituting the term *something* for unknown words and inferring meaning on the basis of world knowledge or their knowledge of cognates. Similar reading strategies emphasizing the importance of previous knowledge in reading have been used in ESL classrooms by Scott (1985). Hudelson's recent work (1984) represents the other end of a continuum that began in the heyday of structuralism, when nothing was read before it could be spoken. She presents evidence that nonnative children who do not even speak English are able to read English material print which occurs in their environment. This shows the strong effect that background knowledge and the cultural framework have in influencing comprehension. So important is background knowledge in L1 reading that Langer (1984) has developed a word-association test for its assessment, which is a reliable predictor of comprehension.

Studies of Cultural Effects on Children's Reading

Another group of studies focuses on the reading behavior of children who are native speakers of English but represent subcultures. While these studies do not address the additional problems of reading in a foreign language and the interaction of language and content schemata, they do provide a rigorous study of the effect of cultural schemata. Lipson (1983) had 4th, 5th, and 6th graders from Catholic and Jewish backgrounds read two passages based on the religious practices of each group. As in the case of studies of adult readers, she found a significant group by passage interaction. Furthermore, she found that implicit recall, probed recall, and errors also showed a passage by religion interaction. These findings support the claim that cultural background is a factor to be considered in reading. Lipson also studied responses to a text based on a topic about which readers did not have previous information. High levels of inferential recalls and low error rates for this neutral topic led her to propose that the behavior being tapped demonstrated a conflict between the world knowledge the reader already possessed and the information presented in the text, not the absence of the appropriate schema. Presumably, the presence of the relevant schema would not have a strong facilitating effect. In a related study, Lipson (1984) addressed the questions of whether younger children are less proficient readers because they have less prior knowledge than do older readers. She found that if children had inaccurate information about a topic before reading a passage, they were less likely to get it correct on the posttest than if they had no information at all before reading about that topic.

Another study in which religious group membership was the independent variable was conducted by Andersson and Gipe (1984). In a population of 6th graders, they found a strong relationship between cultural group membership and inferential measures for passages with 12 familiar and 12 unfamiliar schemata for each group. In addition, they found that creative children took more risks making inferences. On the basis of these findings and other research, Andersson and Barnitz (1984) stress the importance of building background knowledge through such methods as the *language experience approach*, which provides a perfect match of reading material and students' prior knowledge. The development of the *experience-text-relationship* (Au, 1979), in which experiences that are similar to those in the text are discussed before reading and the relationships are drawn after reading, also facilitates comprehension by accessing related prior knowledge.

A study of black inner-city and white rural 8th graders tapped the background information of the minority students with a text based on a *sounding* episode (Reynolds, Taylor, Steffensen, Shirey, & Anderson, 1982). Sounding is a form of verbal play in which status is established through the use of ritual insults. After reading the text, subjects were asked to write as complete a recall as possible and to rate a number of probe statements according to their convergence with or divergence from the text. White subjects experience the sort of schema interference that has been found in other studies of adults and children. On the recall task, their disambiguations and intrusions were more compatible with a fight than a verbal play scenario, and they tend to rate fight probes as occurring in, or compatible with, the text. On the basis of the recall protocols and the rating of probes, black subjects shared the schema underlying the text and recognized that the episode involved verbal sparring between friends. These studies have provided empirical support for the claim that cultural background knowledge does affect the reading comprehension of children as well as adults. However, it does not address the question of how this phenomenon interacts with language in the case of nonnative readers of English.

In connection with these studies, it should be noted that at least in the case of adults, there does seem to be knowledge of the dominant culture on the part of minority members that makes reading texts about that group nonproblematical. In the cross-cultural study of Indians and Americans (Steffensen et al., 1979), an Indian Moslem and an American Jew volunteered as subjects. After the experiment, both men expressed some concern about knowing and being able to recall details of the rituals of their mainstream cultures. However, their protocols were indistinguishable from those of others from their country. Similar knowledge of the minority culture by adult members of the majority or of one minority culture by a member of a different one would probably not be found because of lack of interaction between two groups. It remains to be seen whether children with their more limited experience in their own culture have similar widespread knowledge.

The most extensive study assessing the reading of children from different cultural backgrounds was conducted by K. S. Goodman and Y. Goodman (1978). They studied eight groups of children; four composed of students who spoke a language other than English as their mother tongue before entering school—Navajo, Samoan, Arabic, and Spanish; the other four groups were composed of students who spoke different dialects of English—Downeast Maine, Appalachian white, rural Black, and Hawaiian Pidgin. Subjects were drawn from grades 2, 4, and 6. Each subject read two stories: One was a standard story, and the other represented more closely the cultural background of the subject's own group. All the children were first asked to retell the story, then answer several open-ended questions which were to provide further evidence of comprehension. The miscues that the readers produced as they read were recorded.

The analysis of the miscues indicated the influence of social context on reading: "the common experience, concepts, interests, views and life-styles of readers with common social and cultural background will also be reflected in how and what people read and what they take from their reading" (Goodman & Goodman, 1978, p. 3). They found that the knowledge and background experiences that readers brought to their reading were related to their construction of the meaning of the text. Furthermore, they found that cultural effect was more pronounced in the higher than in the lower grades, supporting the claim that schema development is correlated with age.

Another study which attempted to assess the impact of cultural background knowledge on L2 readers was carried out by Connor (1983).[1] As in the study by Steffensen et al. (1979), the first part of this study used a complete design: 4th and 5th grade American and ESL Spanish-speaking children read and recalled two stories, each drawing upon the Christmas traditions of one of the cultural backgrounds. Unexpectedly, subjects did not read the familiar passage significantly faster nor did they score significantly better on comprehension questions based on the familiar passage. Connor concluded that length of residency (mean of 6.4 years) may have been a factor in "the apparent fluency of the two cultural traditions" (1983, p. 11). A second study was run with newly arrived children (5 to 18 months of residency) who were 9 to 11 years of age. One group was Hispanic; the other represented a variety of cultures including Turkish, Korean, Japanese, Indonesian, Vietnamese, and Italian. Again, differences in reading time and correct answers were nonsignificant. Connor concludes "that length of residence in the US and general reading ability may be stronger factors in reading comprehension than cultural context of the text" (1983, p. 12). She suggests "the implication for ESL reading instructional practice is that the role of prior cultural background knowledge may not be as important in children's reading comprehension as it has been shown to be in that of adults" (1983, p. 15).

These are rather surprising results and conclusions, given the considerable evidence that congruence of cultural background knowledge with text is a significant factor in comprehension. An examination of the texts and their underlying cultural assumptions throws some light on this situation. According to Connor (1983),

> Christmas in the Anglo culture is typically on one or two days while Christmas celebration in the Hispanic culture goes on for days or weeks. Santa Claus, Christmas trees and flowering plants, Christmas dinners with turkey and stuffing are concepts common for the North American Christmas. In the Hispanic tradition, on the other hand, religious orientation with the manger scene and the midnight Mass are more typical. (p. 6)

In fact, for most Anglo families, Christmas involves far more than one or two days' celebration, and for many, the family manger scene and the Christmas Eve church service are important components of the holiday season. The Hispanic passage would probably not be perceived as extremely foreign by American subjects. As for the Hispanic readers, especially those with long residency in the United States, the American passage describes secular Christmas traditions which are carried into the school and the market place: writing to the North Pole, visiting a department store Santa Claus, and details of decorating a tree. Again, these would not represent exotic, unknown events for ESL students who had been in the US for even one Christmas.

In a second experiment, Connor attempted to control for the effects of long residency and instruction in Hispanic culture and language by using subjects from an English-only school who had arrived more recently than those in the first study. Five Hispanics and ten subjects from other cultures read and were tested on the two passages. Reported t-values were 1.34 for the non-Hispanic subjects and .14 for the Hispanic, nonsignificant at the .05 level. Connor did find that length of residency correlated significantly with non-Hispanic students' scores on the Anglo passage, but not with those on the Hispanic passage. This finding suggests that there was some accommodation to the L2 culture resulting in improved reading scores which should be further investigated.

Following this lead and the fact that the subject matter of the two experimental passages appears to be based on knowledge shared by the two original groups of subjects, Connor's study can be reanalyzed. Consider that there is just one experimental task—understanding and answering questions about two texts with a Christian background. For this new analysis, subjects must be grouped on the dimension of religious background: The one Italian and the five Hispanic students form a Christian background group (C); the Korean, Indonesian, Japanese, Vietnamese, and Turkish subjects form a non-Christian background group (NC). If there is an effect of background knowledge that is being tapped by the experimental task, the C scores would be significantly higher than the NC scores.

An analysis yields means of 9.67 for the C group, 7.22 for the NC group. A one-tail t-test shows this difference to be significant at the $p < .01$ level. This is a robust finding, considering the small number of subjects (15) and the restricted assessment procedure (20 short answer questions on the two passages). Results would be even stronger with a balanced design—passages that were based on a familiar and unfamiliar event for each group. However, what is particularly important about this reanalysis is that it brings the performance of these subjects into line with that of other children and adults participating in the studies reported above and clears up an apparent anomaly in this area of research.

Research Questions

There are a number of research questions that these studies raise in connection with the L2 reading of children. First, what are the limits of schemata interference in children, and does this differ from the behavior found in adults? It has been shown for both mature and young readers that there is interference if the text involves an event or ritual that shows fairly pronounced differences across culture. Such episodes as weddings and bar mitzvahs are best understood if the reader possesses the privileged information of the insider. However, there is a great deal of information that can be conveyed across cultural boundaries that is probably based on human universals rooted in shared biological features, among other things. Where, between these two extremes, does cultural interference in reading become a matter of concern? At what point does a text convey enough different information so that an individual reader cannot handle it through the normal processes of inferencing? The answer to these questions is important in the selection of texts and the way they are taught. It also has implications for giving oral instructions about procedures to be followed (e.g., the delivery of health care), since it has been shown that interference and facilitation also occur in listening behavior. It should be noted that individual differences in inferencing behavior have been related to creativity (Andersson & Gipe, 1984) and to cultural membership (Saracho, 1983). Such findings predict that a creative individual from a tradition that fosters risk taking in reading would perform much better on a text than someone with a low level of creativity from a "more literal" tradition.

The claim has been made that the effect of culture is primarily negative, that is, cultural knowledge can cause interference but has less power to facilitate reading (Lipson, 1983, 1984). The dimensions of this claim must be clarified, for it is certainly the case that elaborations are produced when reading a culturally familiar text that cannot be explained except through the effect of background knowledge. A reader will remember information which was not present in the text but represents culturally appropriate intrusions of the undergirding schema. Furthermore, the Fillmore-Kaye procedure suggests that there are many levels of experience tapped by the individual reading a culturally familiar text. Is this simply an artifact of the method, or is the experience of reading a text based on a familiar culture a richer one than the experience of reading one based on an unknown culture?

Related to this is the separate concern of interest. It has generally been assumed that students of language are very interested in learning about the target culture, and this has been advanced as a strong argument for introducing literature and L2 texts. While this may be true for many university-level students living in English-speaking countries, there is anecdotal evidence, gathered by Steffensen and Colker (1982) in a study of adults with low levels of education (less than 12 grades of school), which suggests that this may not be true for all groups. This is an area that should be systematically examined. It would not be surprising to find that interest varies with dimensions such as cultural membership, age, and educational level.

It seems quite reasonable to predict that children will have less fully articulated schemata for cultural events than adults from the same culture. Goodman and Goodman's research (1978) showing variation over grade levels provides support for the claim that schemata develop over a wide range of experiences and represent the generalized structure which subsumes these particular events. On the basis of their limited experience, children would simply have less from which to generalize. If this does in fact prove to be the case, then it would not be surprising to find a great deal of the cultural information that children do have is stored as specific memories. While a child may lack a schema for funerals, the memory of one attended may be very clear. Such memories have been characterized as episodic by Tulving

(1983). Based on personal experience, episodic memory is very specific and is stored with information about the time and place of acquiring the information. This can be contrasted with semantic memory, which is generalized, abstract, and forms a systematized body of information that is acquired through several sources of information and may not involve direct personal experience.

If children do have less fully articulated schemata and fewer details gathered from experience with and interaction in their culture, then it should be less of a problem to teach them details about the target culture. There would be fewer sources of conflict. While children do not possess generic cultural information, but rather are acquiring the details and building the schemata appropriate for one culture, it may also be the case that their openness and lack of experience make it much easier for them to acquire the details of a different culture.

Conclusion

There is a considerable body of research which shows that the cultural backgrounding of a text is a factor in both L1 and L2 reading. The fact that there has not been a number of similar studies directed to the behavior of young L2 readers probably reflects the widespread belief that children's reading is skewed toward decoding, in which comprehension is less important than learning bottom-up skills. Furthermore, the methodology, often using total or verbatim recall, would appear to be more appropriate for use with adults.

However, the studies that have been concerned with children's L2 reading lead to the prediction that cultural content is a force in reading. A limited number of studies with English-speaking children using texts based on unfamiliar subcultures have demonstrated the same sort of interference and elaboration found with adults. In addition, the emphasis on the language experience approach and the experience-test-relationship is a reflection of practitioners' and researchers' years of experience, which show that children are more proficient when they do not have to acquire a high level of content while learning basic reading skills and strategies.

Durkin (1980) is correct in her view that the process of comprehension depends on and develops schemata. While children should not be forced to read materials that are almost devoid of content, they should also not be expected to develop schemata from the ground up on the basis of their reading. This is a behavior with which even highly proficient readers have only limited success (see Steffensen et al., 1979; Steffensen, 1986). If children who are reading English as a nonnative language are to have the greatest success in this skill and are to reach their level of greatest proficiency as rapidly as possible, then practitioners should adapt their reading instruction and methodologies to that adage that reflects so many years of experience—begin teaching at the point where your students are, not where you would like them to be. There is growing evidence that this applies both to the matter of skills and content in L2 reading.

References

Andersson, B. V., & Barnitz, J.G. (1984). Cross-cultural schemata and reading comprehension instruction. *Journal of Reading, 28,* 102-108.
Andersson, B. V., & Gipe, J. P. (1984). Creativity as a mediating variable in inferential reading comprehension. *Reading Psychology, 4,* 313-325.
Au, K. H., (1979). Using the experience-text-relationship method with minority children. *The Reading Teacher, 32,* 677-679.
Barrera, R. B. (1983). Bilingual reading in the primary grades: Some questions about questionable views and practices. In T. H. Escobedo (Ed.), *Early childhood bilingual education* (pp. 164-184). New York: Teachers College.
Carrell, P. L. (1981). Culture-specific schemata in L2 comprehension. In R. A. Orem & J. F. Haskell (Eds.), *Selected papers from the Ninth Illinois TESOL/BE annual convention and the first midwest TESOL conference* (pp. 123-132). Chicago: Illinois TESOL/BE.
Clarke, M. A., & Silberstein, S. (1977). Toward a realization of psycholinguistic principles in the ESL reading class. *Language Learning, 27,* 135-154.
Connor, U. (1983). *Cultural schemata and ESL children's reading comprehension.* Unpublished manuscript.
Cziko, G. A. (1978). Differences in first and second-language reading: The use of syntactic, semantic and discourse constraints. *Canadian Modern Language Review, 34,* 473-489.
Cziko, G. A. (1980). Language competence and reading strategies: A comparison of first- and second-language oral reading errors. *Language Learning, 30,* 101-116.
Durkin, D. (1978). What classroom observations reveal about reading comprehension instruction. *Reading Research Quarterly, 14,* 481-522.
Durkin, D. (1980). *What is the value of the new interest in reading comprehension?* (Reading Education Report No. 19). Urbana: University of Illinois, Center for the Study of Reading.
Eaton, A. J. (1983). The oral reading miscues of field-dependent and field-independent Mexican American children. In T. H. Escobedo (Ed.), *Early childhood bilingual education* (pp. 222-238). New York: Teachers College.
Fillmore, C. J. (1981). Ideal readers and real readers. In D. Tannen (Ed.), *Analyzing discourse: Text and talk.* (Georgetown University Roundtable on Languages and Linguistics 1981) (pp. 248-270). Washington, DC: Georgetown University.
Freedle, R., & Hall, W. S. (1975). *Culture and language: The Black American experience.* Washington, DC: Hemisphere Publishing.
Goodman, K. S. (1965). *A linguistic study of cues and miscues in reading.* Arlington, VA: ERIC Document Reproduction Service.
Goodman, K. S. (1967). Reading: A psycholinguistic guessing game. *Journal of the Reading Specialist, 6,* 126-135.
Goodman, K. S., & Goodman, Y. (1978). *Reading of American children whose language is a stable rural dialect or a language other than English* (Final Report). Washington, DC: National Institute of Education.
Hewitt, G. (1980). A preliminary study of pupils' reading difficulties. *Educational Review, 32,* 231-244.

Hosenfeld, C. (1984). Case studies of ninth grade readers. In J. C. Alderson & A. H. Urquhart (Eds.), *Reading in a foreign language* (pp. 231-244). New York: Longman.
Hudelson, S. (1984). Kan yu rit an rayt Ingles: Children become literate in English as a second language. *TESOL Quarterly, 18,* 221-238.
Langer, J. (1984). Examining background knowledge and text comprehension. *Reading Research Quarterly, 19,* 468-481.
Lipson, M. Y. (1983). The influence of religious affiliation on children's memory for text information. *Reading Research Quarterly, 18,* 448-457.
Lipson, M. Y. (1984). Some unexpected issues in prior knowledge and comprehension. *The Reading Teacher, 37,* 760-764.
Lopez, S. H. (1977). Children's use of contextual clues in reading Spanish. *The Reading Teacher, 38,* 735-740.
Reynolds, R. E., Taylor, M., Steffensen, M. S., Shirey, L. L., & Anderson, R. C. (1982). Cultural schemata and reading comprehension. *Reading Research Quarterly, 17,* 357-366.
Saracho, O. N. (1983). Cognitive style and Mexican American children's perceptions of reading. In T. H. Escobedo (Ed.), *Early childhood bilingual education* (pp. 201-221). New York: Teachers College.
Scott, M. (April, 1985). *Metacognitive training: Techniques for developing student reading awareness.* Paper presented at the 19th Annual TESOL Convention, New York.
De Silva, A. D. (1983). The Spanish reading process and Spanish-speaking Mexican American children. In T. H. Escobedo (Ed.), *Early childhood bilingual education.* (pp. 185-200). New York: Teachers College.
Steffensen, M. S. (1986) Register, cohesion and cross-cultural reading comprehension. *Applied Linguistics, 7,* 71-85.
Steffensen, M. S., & Colker, L. (1982). Intercultural misunderstanding about health care: Recall of descriptions of illness and treatment. *Social Science and Medicine, 16,* 1949-1954.
Steffensen, M. S., Joag-dev, C., & Anderson, R. C. (1979). A cross-cultural perspective on reading comprehension. *Reading Research Quarterly, 15,* 10-29.
Tulving, E. (1983). *Elements of episodic memory.* New York: Oxford University.

Author's Notes

I wish to thank Gary Cziko for his help and valuable comments.

Footnote

[1]The Connor study has not been published. The following discussion is included at the author's request.

Comments on Steffensen

Liz Hamp-Lyons

The University of Michigan

Steffensen's paper, focusing as it does on two relatively neglected areas of second language reading research—cultural influences and children's reading—is particularly welcome. Most reading research has been carried out with adults in the first language. Research into children's reading has been mainly in the first language and has been more psycholinguistic than sociolinguistic. Thus Steffensen is able to review the small number of relevant studies in some detail.

In forming conclusions based on reports of the type Steffensen discusses, it is particularly important to be clear what is intended by the terms *read* and *comprehension*. Readers approach reading in different ways and expect different outcomes based on individual differences of learning style, personality, and interest as well as on differences of culture and subculture. In the same way there can be no such thing as comprehension in any sense of a fixed, nonnegotiable meaning for a text. Since comparative studies of the kinds described in the paper necessitate the forming of judgments about whether the text has been "comprehended," and by extension therefrom whether the text has been "read," it is critical to know the exact research method and assumptions in order to make one's own interpretations. Clearly, this is not possible in a review paper such as Steffensen's and the concerned reader must go for expansion to the primary sources.

It is generally accepted that the use of background knowledge to get sense from a text is a top-down strategy. Steffensen tells us, on the basis of the studies she reviews, that "the strategies readers use therefore appear to be related to their level of reading competence" and that top-down strategies are associated with (comparatively) fluent readers. Later, however, she reports Hudelson's (1984) work which showed that nonnative children who are nonspeakers of English can read English print when it appears "in their environment," and suggests that this shows the strong effect of culture and background knowledge. If this is not to be seen as self-contradictory, we must interpret it as meaning that these naive readers of English use their native language top-down strategies to impose sense on unfamiliar lexis— which just happens to be English. This leaves us with the generalization that readers will use the highest level strategies open to them to make sense of what they read. Only when the top-level strategies do not seem to succeed will they resort to lower level strategies. Such a generalization permits us to reconcile the findings of Hudelson with those of Cziko (1978, 1980). It also explains Lipson's (1984) finding that inaccurate background information distorts comprehension more than no information.

A point of particular interest was made in reporting on Lipson's (1983) work. Lipson suggested that there was a conflict between the reader's background knowledge and the information in the text, leading to anomie or rejection of the alien cultural content. Such a rejection, if it indeed occurred, could only impair comprehension. This is of particular interest to the classroom teacher, who is always looking for ways to aid comprehension. It suggests that the teacher must tread very warily in selecting reading texts, especially when integration into the mainstream culture is one of the objectives of the curriculum. One of the research questions Steffensen puts forward is whether learners of all ages, educational levels, and cultural backgrounds wish to be taught about the culture(s) of native English speakers. It has been argued (Hamp-Lyons, 1983; Kachru, 1984) that they do not. It would be particularly interesting to research Steffensen's question as to whether children, having (perhaps) less fully developed cultural knowledge, would be more open to learning the schemata of a different culture. This is not, however, a question specifically of reading research, but of second language acquisition research in general.

Returning to the more limited question of cultural influences on children's reading in a second language, the weight of data does seem to suggest that requirements made upon cultural background knowledge influence children's success in comprehending text in the second language, as they do for adults. But since there is nothing to be done to remove such requirements from the second language reading children must do, other solutions to the problems thus raised must be found. Such solutions are to be found through an open approach to cultural information in the classroom, in which subcultures are valued, discussed, and read about as is the mainstream culture and through an approach to reading which favors interpretation rather than the strait jacket of right and wrong answers. With such an approach children are encouraged to interact with other readers to share and evaluate alternative interpretations and to write in personal response to a text. Clearly there are some implications for materials in terms of both content and methodology, some of which are suggested in Steffensen's conclusion, and this in itself forms a useful area for future research.

References

Cziko, G. A. (1978). Differences in first-and second-language reading: The use of syntactic, semantic and discourse constraints. *Canadian Modern Language Review, 34,* 473-489.

Cziko, G. A. (1980). Language competence and reading strategies. A comparison of first-and second-language oral reading errors. *Language learning, 30,* 101-116.

Hamp-Lyons, L. (1983). Motivation for learning English as a world language: Integrative and instrumental. *World Language English, 2*, 3.
Hudelson, S. (1984). Kan yu rit an rayt Ingles: Children become literate in English as a second language oral reading errors. *TESOL Quarterly, 18*, 221-238.
Kachru, B. B. (1984). World Englishes and the teaching of English to non-native speakers: Contexts, attitudes, and concerns. *TESOL Newsletter, 17*, 25-26.
Lipson, M. Y. (1983). The influence of religious affiliation on children's memory for text information. *Reading Research Quarterly, 18*, 448-457.
Lipson, M. Y. (1984). Some unexpected issues in prior knowledge and comprehension. *The Reading Teacher, 37*, 760-764.

Reading in a Second Culture

Kate J. Parry

Hunter College, City University of New York

Reading in a Second Culture

In Nigeria the West African School Certificate (WASC) is taken as the primary index of the country's educational achievement; and there is general agreement that, of all the parts of this exam, the English language section is the most important (Ndahi, 1977). There is good reason for this assessment, as English, although a second language to most Nigerians, is the medium of the country's education, administration, and much of its commerce. Without a good passing grade in English on the WASC, a secondary school leaver cannot expect to go far.

There is, therefore, considerable public dismay over the fact that the WASC English language results are generally poor, and especially so in the north of the country. In Gongola State, for example, a survey done in 1980 reported that only 25% of the students in the 13 schools considered secured a pass. There has, however, been no systematic study of why the results are so poor, and of what, in particular, the linguistic and cognitive problems to be overcome are.

The research, of which this paper reports a part, was designed to find an answer to these questions and concentrated on reading for two reasons. First, there is general agreement among teachers and students that the reading sections of the English language test are the most difficult and that these sections are responsible for the high failure rate. Second, since there are few native speakers of English in the country, and English radio and television programs are limited, students' access to the language—and to the culture that it represents—is determined primarily by their ability to read. Of crucial importance, therefore, is the question: What do the students understand from what they read? Is it the same as that which native speakers understand from reading the same text?

The model of reading on which the study was based is an interactive one. There is general agreement that true reading, as opposed to decoding, involves the perception of meaning at different levels ranging from the lowest, individual graphemes, to the highest, the text as a whole. There is, however, some controversy as to how these levels of meaning are integrated in the reader's mind (Ulijn, 1980). Some argue that reading is a *bottom-up* process: graphemes are perceived as forming words, words as forming sentences, sentences as forming paragraphs, and so on (Gough, 1972). Others argue that the process is *top-down:* the reader starts with a general idea or schema, derived from previously acquired knowledge of what should be in the text and uses this schema in perceiving and interpreting graphic cues (Goodman, 1967; Smith, 1982). I would suggest, following Rumelhart (1977), Ulijn (1980), that there is in fact an interaction between the levels. The reader starts with the perception of graphic cues, but as soon as these are recognized as familiar, schemata derived from both linguistic knowledge and knowledge of the world in general are brought into play. The proportion of graphic cues that must be perceived varies with individual texts and with individual readers according to the difficulty of the former and the knowledge and confidence in that knowledge of the latter.

A number of studies have shown that high-level schemata are as important in L2 reading as in L1 (Johnson, 1982; Hudson, 1982; Alderson & Urquhart, 1983). In addition, it is likely in second language reading that the appropriate schemata will be lacking, as the language and the text are products of a culture alien to the student. Carrell and Eisterhold (1983) provide a number of examples of how texts which are perfectly transparent to people familiar with North American culture present severe problems to those who do not have this familiarity, even when all the individual linguistic items are known.

The cultural difference between text and reader is particularly marked for ESL readers who do not have European backgrounds (Coady, 1979). Such is the case with the students who have to take the WASC English language examination: Their physical and social environments are totally diffferent from those which formed the English language, and which thereby inform the tests with which the students have to deal. The study was an attempt to find out how these broader cultural differences interact with particular linguistic deficiencies to produce answers in the WASC tests that are completely off-target. Passages were selected from the exams of the last 10 years and were given to a group of 20 students who were in their final year at secondary school. The answers were analyzed, and the students were interviewed in an attempt to elicit identifiable difficulties and to determine what the students thought the substance of the texts was about.

The study was conducted with students from Saint Peter's Seminary, Yola, which is in Gongola State in northeastern Nigeria. St. Peter's is a minor seminary, or a secondary school run by the Roman Catholic Mission, for boys considering priesthood. Students come from places where there are Catholic mission stations. Such stations have been established only among peoples who were not Muslim and who were outside the cultural mainstream of the Western Sudan. They were small-scale, isolated societies with cultures based on simple technology and a self-sufficient and undifferentiated agricultural economy. The bonds within and distinctions between different groups within these societies are determined primarily by ties of kinship; and the identity of each people as a whole is expressed in its own language, as well as in its own religion and mythology.

The 20 students who participated in this project belong to 12 different peoples and have 12 different native languages; however, they all speak Hausa, the lingua franca of Northern Nigeria. With several of them speaking one or two other local languages as well, they have 23 African languages among them. Of all these languages only Hausa was written (in Arabic script) before the present century and these students are not very familiar with its written form. This fact has an important effect on their concept of meaning (c.f. Olson, 1977); they have little acquaintance with linguistic devices that have developed through writing which are peculiarly characteristic of languages such as English (Havranek, 1929). These students are reading in a second culture in two senses: Not only is the physical and social environment that they know totally different from that which is reflected in the lexical structure of English, but in learning to read, they are moving from an oral to a literate culture (Goody & Watt, 1968; Goody, 1977; Ong, 1982).

Because of this cultural dimension, the project was initiated with a passage with fairly accessible content (c.f. Paulston & Bruder, 1976).

> Read the following passage carefully and answer the questions on it.
>
> Two of the most *attractive* up-river tribes of North-West Borneo are the Sea Dayaks and the Land Dayaks. They obtained these names from the British who first came into contact with them; the former *on account* of their skill in navigation on the sea along the coast, and the latter because they were inexpert boatmen and few of them could paddle or swim.
>
> Though in facial appearance and language the two races differ *sharply*, they are alike in their mild temperament, obedience to authority, willingness to work hard and honesty. So trustworthy, also, are those that live in their traditional environment, that their word can safely be taken as their *bond*.
>
> The Dayaks are very fond of their parents, brothers, sisters and children, and often a strong *attachment* exists between man and wife which lasts for life. Each man has only one wife, and, if for any reason the union has to be *dissolved*, he appeals to his parents and the village chief for permission to divorce. This is usually agreed to, provided that *adequate* compensation is paid to the parties that have borne the cost of bringing the partners together.
>
> (a) Give for each of the following a single word that could take its place in the passage:
>
>   (i) attractive,
>   (ii) on account,
>   (iii) sharply,
>   (iv) bond,
>   (v) attachment,
>   (vi) adequate.

(b) Give three nouns that denote three good qualities of the Dayaks.
(c) State three ways in which the two tribes differ.
(d) Give:
   (i) one adjective to describe the kind of marriage system common among the Dyaks (sic);
   (ii) one noun in place of *parents, brothers, sisters and children;*
   (iii) one verb in place of *dissolved.*

These two tribes are described in much the same terms as one might use to describe those of Northern Nigeria. Lexical difficulties were expected. Of the 191 words in the passage, 22 are outside the 2000 most commonly used in English (West, 1964); however, if the students were prepared to make inferences from context, they had a fair chance of guessing the correct meanings. At the syntactic level one or two difficulties were anticipated. The second sentence is very long, and the second half of it is highly elliptical. In addition, the reference items *the former* and *the latter* seemed likely to cause confusion. Finally, the metalanguage used in questions (b) and (d) could potentially create difficulties, and students might not understand all the answers, but they would at least have a good general understanding of the passage.

The problems that actually arose were different from those anticipated. There were only three words—*facial, temperament,* and *compensation*—that more than one or two students claimed never to have heard. However, there were many other words that they had heard, but they were either uncertain of their meaning or had difficulty in relating the meaning to this context. This was apparent in their answers to question (a). Faced with this task they seem to have adopted one of five different strategies:

(1) Simply give up and leave the space blank.
(2) Supply a metalinguistic description of the word's function.
(3) Give a word that collocates with those in the immediate context, but does not have any particular association with the word for which it is supposed to be substituted.
(4) Give the meaning as learned in a different context (a "dictionary" meaning), without trying to modify it to fit this particular passage.
(5) Work from the already learned dictionary meaning but interpret the word in the light of the surrounding text and of one's knowledge of the world in general.

Strategy 5 is what one is supposed to use (Smith, 1982). When reading in a second culture, it may often not be successful.

These strategies are exemplified in the answers given to question (a, i), as words which might be substituted for *attractive.* No student claimed never to have heard this word, but four could not answer the question. One used

Strategy 2, saying that *attractive* was an adjective. One seemed to adopt Strategy 3 in answering *important*, but he modified this in the interview to *beautiful*. This latter answer seems to be a product of Strategy 4, derived from the students' having heard *attractive* in collocation with *girl* or, in the examples they gave themselves, with *clothes*. Three others gave answers of this type, supplying the words *good-looking, pleasing,* and *liked,* and the four who could not answer gave similar answers in the interview (which suggests that they were trying to use Strategy 5. Another variant on this strategy was to work from the dictionary meaning of the verb *attract* and its collocation with *attention*. This produced *noticeable* and *having power*. One, however, realized that this would not work: "It doesn't make sense as *attractive*," he complained. "This *attractive* is what draws attention . . . for example, when you went to the market, when you are just walking around, when you see how—how beautiful [are the] clothes. . . "

The answer that such students arrived at was *impressive*—preferred to *lovely*, as one of them said, because "*impressive* sank into the heart . . . you will not forget the appearance." Or *interesting*. The latter was the target response; for although it does not, in native speakers' use correspond to *attractive*, it does in the way in which it is commonly used in Nigeria. (One of the students, when asked to point out something in the room that was interesting said that he thought the carpet was.)

Sharply (1, iii) presented greater difficulties. The boys all knew the word *sharp* and its collocation with *knife, razor,* or *needle*; and those that adopted Strategy 4 accordingly produced *keen* and *with fine cutting*. But most realized that there must be some figurative meaning here. As one of them said: "A sharp or narrow escape or the edge of a knife is very sharp. Here it doesn't have anything to do with a knife. Here it means a little different. . . " The image is obvious enough when one thinks of it, and this was the direction in which 6 of the 15 who gave any answer at all went, supplying *a little, a bit, simply,* or *slightly*. One, however, took the image in quite a different way:

> They differ and they say *sharply* at the end. Now it can also be said that they differ actually . . . It means a lot . . . It's because that . . . *sharp* means something very very—just as needle . . . that's the point, the end.

Figurative extensions of meaning can be almost as arbitrary a matter of convention as are assignations of particular sets of phonemes to particular referents.

The difficulty with *sharply* interacts with another lexical problem, namely, the word *facial*. There were four students who said that they did not know this word, and one other mispronounced it when reading aloud, suggesting that he too had never heard it. This affects Question C, which asks for ways in which the two tribes differ. The response, amongst these five, was either to give no answer to C at all, or to seek an answer elsewhere in the text. One found it in the first paragraph. His response to C was:

> The Sea Dayaks are skillful in navigation
> The Land Dayaks are inexpert boatman
> A few of the Land Dayaks can swim or paddle.

The fact that he was not sure of *facial,* together with his interpretation of *sharply* as "a little" seems to have so diminished the force of "although in facial appearance and language the two races difffer sharply" that he ignored the clause altogether.

But this interpretation is not solely the result of the lexis. It is clear from this student's response, and from that of seven others, that the difference in the Sea and Land Dayaks' ways of life was very salient to them, even though the word *differ* does not appear in the paragraph in which the point is made. One of them, in interview, discoursed on the point at length:

> The first answer is that the Land Dayaks lived on land, while the Sea Dayaks lived on water. And also the land Dayaks are farmers, when the Sea Dayaks are fishermen . . . Because [the Land Dayaks] live on land. And since they have sufficient land they farm in order to feed themselves.

Here the student is bringing a great deal of his own knowledge to bear on the text.

The two other students who did not know *facial*—who, incidentally, gave no answer at all for *sharply*—gave some variation of the clause "They are alike in their mild temperament, willingness to work hard and honesty" for an answer to C, which was even more off-target. Here it seems that the lexical problem interacted with a morphological one. One student who gave this answer plainly thought that *alike* meant "unlike": "I can say that Form 2 and 5 are alike," he said, "because they're not in the same class. There are just things that Form 5 can do they cannot do." Another said: "The two races differ. That is the two tribes are different," and when asked in what respects they were different he replied, "They are alike in their obedience to authority, willingness to work hard and honesty."

The lexical difficulties also create and interact with difficulties in understanding the rhetorical structure of the whole text. Consider the first sentence:

> Two of the most attractive up-river tribes of North-West Borneo are the Sea Dayaks and the Land Dayaks.

An explanation of the names follows, linked to the preceding sentence by the reference item *these*. The next paragraph picks up the theme suggested by *attractive*. It gives a catalogue of the Dayaks' virtues and explains why the writer describes them this way. *Attractive,* as we have seen, is not understood by many of these students in the writer's sense. If it means "good-looking" in this case, one would expect a different development of the passage. It is not so surprising then that all but two of the students missed the answer to Question B, especially since they could not say what *quality* meant, nor did they have enough knowledge of syntax to be able to identify *nouns* with confidence. This is an interesting point, in view of the oral nature of all the students' other languages. In such languages general abstract nouns, such as *quality* are unlikely to develop (Goody, 1977). This is more true of metalinguistic terms like *noun*.[1] They had all been taught in primary school that a noun was "the name of a place, person, or thing," and they trotted out this definition without hesitation. A couple of them took it seriously, supplying, in answer to (b) "names" of persons—that is, *parents, brothers*, and *sisters*.

A more interesting point arises from the students' interpretation of *bond*. Everyone claimed to know this word. Most remembered having learned it in history lessons the previous year when they had studied the Gold Coast Bond of 1846, a treaty that was made between the British Company of Merchants and the Gold Coast chiefs. Seven, accordingly, gave *agreement* as their answer for A, iv, while four others gave variants of the same idea: *treaty, alliance, unity, covenant*. Of the nine others, six gave similar answers orally in the interview. Clearly this word represented another idea which was salient for them.

The interpretation of *bond* as "agreement" or "unity" does interesting things to the clause "their word can be taken as their bond." One boy took *word* in its dictionary sense, as referring to the word *Dayaks*, and so he said that this statement meant: "Only *Land* and *Sea* differentiate them. Because it is all *Dayaks*." Another took *word* at a higher level of generality, to mean "language": "Their language they're taking as their bond," he said, thus showing, as he did also in his answer to Question C, that he had missed the point that "in facial appearance and language the two races differ sharply." Both these boys may have been thinking of peoples they know, such as the Town Fulani and the Bush Fulani, who speak the same language and share the same name but who have very different ways of life.

A larger group of students took the word *word* to mean "speech," as the writer intends, but it was the speech of the community that they were thinking of, rather than that of individuals. One of these boys, for instance, said, "They take their word as an agreement to each and every one of them—and they obey their authority, they work hard, and they are honest to each other." Another said, "If they say something, for example, the leaders if they say something, or the two Land and Sea Dayaks . . . they do the thing equally, they do the thing the same." And yet another said ". . . their word, when they say it, will be taken as the agreement [of] the village people . . . with their king [or when I pointed out that the king is not mentioned] between foreigners and the villagers."

So powerful was this interpretation of *bond* that several students carried it through to the end of the passage, ignoring the rhetorical shift signalled by the beginning of the third paragraph, and the new topic introduced by "each man has only one wife." One boy, for example, said that the word *union* referred to ". . . the coming together of two tribes, or agreement between the people themselves"; and so too, to his mind, did the word *attachment*. He accordingly gave *attachment*, in answer to Question B, as one of the good qualities of the Dayaks. "Because," he said, "It describes the people as . . . one nation, so . . . their quality is that they're joined together . . . because if there is no attachment . . . there will be no existence between them." Here again, one can see an interaction between the students' interpretations at the lexical and rhetorical levels, for their answers to Question A, v, show that their interpretation of *attachment* was also a limited one. Most of them gave *connection* in its place, working from the dictionary meaning of the related verb, *attach;* thus, the component of "affection" was lost to them.

Another factor in the interaction was the students' experience of political and social reality. They come from a part of the world where there is a multiplicity of different ethnic groups, the rivalry between which is a major concern in Nigerian politics. Loyalty and coherence within these groups are highly valued. Their importance can be seen even in the school context where students form tribal unions to engage in common activities. With such a social background the boys are naturally inclined to interpret this passage in terms of tribal rather than marital relations.

This is more than a simple failure to understand. It might be more appropriately described as misinterpretation. The starting point is the lexis. The words are not unknown, for the most part, but the students have come across them only in limited contexts and they do not know how extended their reference may or may not be. For words that relate to salient ideas, like *bond* and *attachment*, they tend to give too narrow an interpretation. This leads to a distortion of other words, like *word*. Through this process they gather sufficient information to activate schemata, but these, though relevant, do not exactly match what the writer has in mind.

In applying these schemata the students are not restrained by the syntactic and rhetorical cues that are supplied by the text. They do not, for example, use the contrast suggested by *though* when they are trying to figure out the meaning of *sharply*. They ignore the paragraph divisions, so that it is possible for them to see false cohesive ties, like that between *their bond* and *the union*. This is not because they do not know these syntactic and rhetorical devices, but rather because the schemata activated by the lexis are overridingly powerful.

It may also be that in their approach to this text the students are using still higher level schemata, concerned with the nature of meaning itself. It has already been said that they come from various ethnic groups, and few of them share the same first language. For much of the time, they are using a second language, usually when they are speaking Hausa amongst themselves, and they may well not be using it accurately. It is more productive, in such circumstances, to think about the meaning of speakers rather than of words and sentences, and to make maximum use of pragmatic and paralinguistic cues. In an oral culture this approach to meaning is entirely appropriate (Olson, 1977), but it is not the approach of the literate culture that this comprehension test represents.

What can be done about these problems? It seems that more attention must be paid to lexis. One approach might be to arrange reading material around particular themes as suggested by Krashen (1981), so that the same lexical items are seen within a short period in a variety of different contexts. Another possibility is to have students examine dictionary entries on key items in reading passages as a prereading activity, noting the alternative definitions and the citations given. It may also be useful to do work on lexical paradigms, studying which words may be substituted for which in particular contexts, and seeing where and why such substitutions will not work.

Students such as these must learn to pay closer attention to syntactic and rhetorical cues. It is particularly important that they appreciate the constraints imposed by different types of conjunction and connective, such as those that are additive and those that are contrastive (Halliday & Hasan, 1976). Both cloze tests and sentence completion exercises could be used for this purpose, preferably based on the students' own writing so that the interaction with lexical problems is minimized.

Finally, to deal with problems at the schematic level, it is most important as teachers to listen to our students (Carrell & Eisterhold, 1983). We should be wary of judging them as unthinking or stupid when they fail to produce target responses in reading tests. The students represented in this study performed abysmally on this reading test (the average score was 19%), and yet it can be seen from what they said in the interview that they were being both active and intelligent in seeking an interpretation of the passage. The problem is that we are asking a great deal of them. Even in passages on familiar subject matter a new language presupposes different attitudes and associations. The inferences which students must make are all too likely to lead them astray.

References

Alderson, J. C., & Urquhart, A. (1983, March). This test is unfair: I'm not an economist. Paper presented at the 17th Annual TESOL Convention, Toronto.
Carrell, P. L., & Eisterhold, J. (1983). Schema theory and ESL reading pedagogy. *TESOL Quarterly, 17*, 553-573.
Coady, J. (1979). A psycholinguistic model of the ESL reader. In R. Mackey, B. Barkman, & R. R. Jordan (Eds.), *Reading in a second language* (pp. 5-12). Rowley, MA: Newbury House.
Goodman, K. S. (1967). Reading: a psycholinguistic guessing game. *Journal of The Reading Specialist, 4*, 13-26.

Goody, J., & Watt. (1968). The consequences of literacy. In J. Goody (Ed.), *Literacy in traditional societies* (pp. 27-68). Cambridge: Cambridge University Press.

Goody, J. (1977). *The domestication of the savage mind*. Cambridge: Cambridge University Press.

Gough, P. B. (1972). One second of reading. *Visible Language, 6*, 291-320.

Halliday, M., & Hasan, R. (1976). *Cohesion in English*. New York: Longman.

Havranek, B. (1929). Influence de la fonction de la langue litteraire sur la structure phonologique et grammaticale du Tcheque litteraire. Travaux du cercle linguistique de Prague I. In *A Prague school reader in linguistics*, Josef Vachek (Ed.) (1964), 252-69. Bloomington, IN: Indiana University Press.

Hudson, T. (1982). The effects of induced schemata on the "short circuit" in L2 reading: Non-decoding factors in L2 reading performance. *Language Learning, 32*, 1-31.

Johnson, P. (1982). Effects on reading comprehension of building backgound knowledge. *TESOL Quarterly, 16*, 503-516.

Krashen, S. D. (1981). The case for narrow reading. *TESOL Newsletter, 15*, 23.

Ndahi, K. S. (1977). The place of grammar in the teaching of English. *The Nigerian Language Teacher, 1*, 18-23.

Olson, D. R. (1977). From utterance to text: the bias of language in speech and writing. *Harvard Educational Review, 47*, 257-81.

Ong, W. J. (1982). *Orality and literacy: the technologizing of the word*. New York: Methuen.

Paulston, C. B., & Bruder, M. N. (1976). *Teaching English as a second language: techniques and procedures*. Cambridge, MA: Winthrop.

Rumelhart, D. E. (1977). Toward an interactive model of reading. In S. Dornic (Ed.), *Attention and performance, Vol. 6* (pp. 573-603). New York: Academic Press.

Smith, F. (1982). *Understanding reading*. New York: Holt, Rinehart, and Winston.

Ulijn, J. (1980). Foreign-language reading research: Recent trends and future prospects. *Journal of Research in Reading, 3*, 17-37.

West, M. P. (1964). *A general service list of English words, with semantic frequencies and a supplementary word-list for the writing of popular science and technology*. London: Longman.

Author's Notes

I should like to thank the Right Reverend Patrick Sheehan, O.S.A., Bishop of Yola, and the late Reverend Father Damian Loughran, O.S.A., former Rector of Saint Peter's Seminary, for the opportunity to pursue this project; the boys who were in Form 5 at Saint Peter's in 1983-1984 for their cooperation in doing the tests and coming to interviews; and Patrick Cummins and Ann Raimes for their comments on the present paper.

Comments on Parry

Mary Lee Field

Wayne State University

The recurring theme in Parry's work, and one that has broader application in the field of reading research, is the different assumptions about meaning and comprehension which exist in oral cultures and in literate cultures. Parry illustrates how her students were caught in a double bind: having to read and perform in a second (or third) language and having to function according to the assumptions and expectations of a literate culture rather than an oral one. That double bind has been the same for a number of groups, including Hmong and other South Asian refugees, and a variety of African nationalities. However, the nature of the differences between oral and literate cultures is still being hotly debated.

The works cited by Parry, including Ong, Olsen, and Goody, establish the parameters of the debate, but the issues are not settled. There were lively exchanges on this topic at the Conference on College Composition and Communication (CCCC) in the spring of 1985. How much difference is there between oral and literate cultures? Is there an element of discrimination in the differences which scholars have catalogued and argued? What assumptions about reading, about recognizing rhetorical structures, about meaning and understanding are inherently dfferent?

Parry's comment that the students appeared more concerned with "the meaning of speakers" than with the comprehension of words and sentences is at the heart of the issue. The assumptions that literate teachers make when they devise a reading comprehension test are possibly far from the assumptions that someone from a nonliterate culture would make about understanding or comprehending a passage. The students, of course, are aware that they are engaged in reading, not listening to an oral presentation. But the transfer of their own oral culture techniques and strategies to that reading exercise is totally unconscious and natural. Cross cultural transfer occurs in learning patterns, ways of solving problems, and ways of processing meaning. Because these processes are unconscious, they are particularly difficult to identify and monitor.

Thus, teachers need to become more sensitive to the ways that our testing instruments reflect the assumptions of literate cultures. Asking for comparisons of the two tribes is an innocent and useful exercise but it is also based on rhetorical patterns of comparison and contrast which are generally accepted by English speakers and other Westerners as basic strategies in manipulating language. Is that true in the oral traditions of the students in Parry's class? Is comparison and contrast a method they would use to question a friend about a narrative that they had not heard? Is definition also a device used in that culture? If not, what methods would they use?

Schema theory researchers have already begun to identify some of the differences, and their work helps the classroom teacher recognize cultural transfers. Parry comments that students "must learn to pay closer attention to syntactic and rhetorical cues." Indeed, teachers can help students become aware, not only of rhetorical cues but also of essential differences between oral and literate approaches to the word, the story, and the meaning. Making these cognitive patterns explicit helps students understand their own ways of working and thinking—thus making them more able to compare methods and to employ the devices of other "cultures."

Schema theory researchers still have unexplored territory in oral/literate schemata to map and analyze. Their analyses, combined with work like Parry's which integrates reading theory with data from classroom experiments, will give us a clearer understanding of cultural differences in the relationships both between reader and text, and between listener and narrative. Then, we will have better tools to bridge the differences between the two cultures and provide the students with the best ways to function in both.

General Language Competence and Adult Second Language Reading

Joanne Devine

Skidmore College

General Language Competence and Adult Second Language Reading

There is a general assumption in much ESL pedagogy that reading achievement in a second language is severely restricted by low proficiency in that language. In my own experience of teaching ESL for 5 years, reading instruction was often delayed entirely until students reached a desired level of overall language proficiency. The reasoning, of course, was that until a minimal level of language competency was achieved, students would not benefit from reading instruction. When beginning level students were put into reading classes, attention usually focused on the development of skills which would eventually figure prominently in "real" reading—vocabulary recognition, sound-letter correspondence (pronunciation drills), and fluency in the structural features of the second language (L2). It should be noted that it is undoubtedly easier to teach these skills, especially at lower proficiency levels, than it is to teach reading—a process which involves the complex interaction of both linguistic and nonlinguistic abilities. However, even at more advanced reading levels in ESL programs, classroom activities have typically emphasized language instruction rather than reading instruction (Eskey, 1973). The assumption has been that until these vocabulary items and grammatical structure from the target language are mastered, efforts to understand written texts in that language will be futile.

The restrictive impact of low L2 language proficiency on reading performance has been a recurring theme in research into second language reading. In the most frequently cited research, Clarke (1980) studied the strategies of low language proficiency "good" and "poor" readers (as determined by performance on cloze tests) reading in their native Spanish and English. He found that when reading in their native Spanish, the poor readers relied more on syntactic cues and less on semantic cues than did the good readers. A close look at a good reader's and a poor reader's strategies as they read in English, however, presented a different picture. The good reader and the poor reader seemed to use syntactic information almost equally, and the good reader's advantage in using semantic cues dramatically declined. In other words, when reading in L2 the good reader performed very much like the poor reader, leading Clarke to conclude,

> Limited language proficiency appears to exert a powerful effect on the behaviors utilized by the readers ... the role of language proficiency may be greater than has previously been assumed; apparently limited control over the language "short circuits" the

good reader's system, causing him/her to revert to poor reader strategies when confronted with a difficult or confusing task in the second language. (p. 206)

Cziko (1978, 1980) compared the reading strategies of limited and advanced English language proficiency French students reading in English with those of native speakers. His findings correspond with those of Clarke. Specifically he found that lower proficiency readers employ poor reading strategies, such as attempting to reproduce exactly the orthographic features of text words. These low language proficiency readers also evidenced relatively few insertions and deletions in their oral reading, again suggesting that they employ a strategy of faithful repetition of the printed text in their reading. On the other hand, advanced English proficiency French subjects tended to behave very much like native English speakers when reading in English, demonstrating a sensitivity to syntactic, semantic, and discourse cues in the text. Cziko concludes that reader strategies are related to competence level in the language. Lower proficiency readers appear to rely on bottom-up strategies for processing information in a text, whereas native and advanced proficiency readers rely on both graphic and contextual cues, as well as more general nontextual information that might be referred to as higher level schemata (both bottom-up and top-down processing).

Hudson (1982), in a study of L2 reading factors, found that advanced language proficiency readers have "more facile and robust networks for fitting meaning than do lower level readers . . . there appear to be differences in the abilities to form schemata from printed input between levels of proficiency" (p. 18). He suggests that the advanced proficiency readers are able to bring more "behind the eyeball" information to bear during reading and are able to minimize reliance on the visual display. Although he agrees with Clarke and Cziko that low language competence may place a linguistic ceiling on achievement in L2 reading, he argues that the ceiling effect can be overridden by a reader's ability to activate appropriate schemata.[1]

The research by Clarke, Cziko, and Hudson converges on a number of important points. Specifically, it suggests that low competence in the target language places a linguistic limit (although not an insurmountable one) on the language learner's ability to read in the target language. It does this, in Clarke's term, by "short circuiting" a reader's system of using available cues. This short circuit forces a reader to revert to less efficient strategies, especially a heavy reliance on graphic (and perhaps syntactic), rather than semantic, information in the text. This close adherence to textual features may also inhibit the reader's ability to activate appropriate higher order schemata. The findings of these researchers provide further insight into the nature of L2 reading and into the need for development of language skills for proficient second language reading, although not necessarily for beginning reading instruction. They do not, however, provide specific information on the dynamic interaction of language proficiency and reading achievement in a second language. An understanding of this interaction is possible only if subjects' general language proficiency level, as well as their reading performance, is examined at regular intervals over the course of a longitudinal study.

The research reported on here is an initial attempt to provide information on the dynamic interaction of language proficiency and reading ability in English for 20 beginning ESL students enrolled in an intensive ESL program. As these subjects were followed over the period of an academic year, records were made of both changes in their reading behavior (see Wilson, 1984) and changes in their overall language proficiency as measured by various testing instruments. It was hoped that a fuller picture of the relationship between general language competency and reading performance in a second language would emerge.

The following general hypotheses concerning the interrelationship between reading performance and general language competency were formulated:

1. There will be a significant, positive correlation between increases in reading proficiency and increases in overall language proficiency.[2]
2. There will be a significant, negative correlation between poor reading strategies (as indicated by a high frequency of oral reading miscues with no or low semantic acceptability, suggesting a strictly bottom-up strategy) and overall language proficiency.

A word of caution is needed at this point. There are a number of problems inherent in attempting to evaluate reading through the use of oral reading samples. Clarke (1979) notes that while oral reading studies are based on the untested assumption that oral reading is equivalent to silent reading, the strategies involved may in fact be very different (see Cunningham & Caplan, 1982). Furthermore, the limited oral language proficiency of many second language readers makes the use of oral summaries or retellings of texts of questionable value for purposes of assessing reading comprehension. For critical discussion of these and other methodological issues involved in the use of oral reading data, see Wixson (1979), Leu (1982), and Allington (1984). Researchers should exercise caution when interpreting research based on oral reading samples; however, as I have argued (Devine 1984), oral reading data often provide the researcher with the only available information on certain aspects of the reading process, such as a reader's reliance on the graphophonic features of a text.

Because efficient, effective reading demands that the reader simultaneously utilize a number of skills from lower level sound/letter recognition to higher order schemata activation rather than a single isolated skill (see Carrell & Eisterhold, 1983), it was further hypothesized that the positive correlations mentioned in Hypothesis 1 would be found only for holistic or integrative measures of language competence (such as cloze, listening, composition, and composite test average scores). Further, negative (or no) correlations would be found between increases in reading proficiency and discrete point tests, such as vocabulary item tests and nonintegrative grammar tests. Two secondary hypotheses are as follows:

3. There will be a significant positive correlation between increased reading proficiency and increased scores on holistic measures of language competence.
4. There will be negative (or no) correlation between increased reading proficiency and increased scores on discrete point measures of language competence.

The Study

The study reported here investigates the reading behavior of 20 beginning level ESL students—13 males and 7 females, ranging in age from 16 to 38—studying at the English Language Center at Michigan State University during the academic year 1982-1983. The subjects were natives of six countries: Iraq, Japan, Mexico, Qatar, Saudi Arabia, and Venezuela. All readers were found to be low English language proficiency at the beginning of the study (see Table 1).

An oral reading sample was collected for each of the 20 readers at intervals of 3 months over the academic year 1982-83, for a total of 3 oral reading samples per subject, and 60 oral reading samples for the entire group. These oral readings were subjected to a *miscue analysis*[3] in order to determine any changes in oral reading performance over the course of the study. The following language proficiency test scores were gathered for each subject upon entrance to the Center and at intervals corresponding to the miscue analyses for the oral readings: grammar, vocabulary, listening, composition, and cloze. Composite scores for grammar-vocabulary-cloze (GVR) tests and a general average for all tests were also recorded. The interaction of these measures of language proficiency and the miscue profiles for the subjects was examined both for each reading and over all readings.

The correlation analysis of reading behavior and language proficiency proceeded as follows. All miscue analyses were completed and checked. The miscue data were computerized to provide mean scores for all readers for the categories of chief interest in the hypotheses being tested: graphic and phonemic similarity, and syntactic and semantic acceptability. Group means were also calculated for the scores on the various language proficiency tests at each of the three data collections. After these two sets of mean scores were obtained, a second computer analysis was run to determine what significant correlations, if any, exist between performance on language proficiency tests and performance in oral reading.

Table 1. Mean Scores for Language Proficiency Tests for Readings 1, 2, and 3 *

TEST	READING 1	READING 2	READING 3
Grammar	40.3	57.8	68.4
Vocabulary	39.6	60.8	67.6
Listening (Aural Comp)	51.6	71.1	77.0
Composition	60.7	68.5	73.9
Cloze	46.5	65.3	74.4
GVR **	42.1	61.1	70.2
Average	51.4	66.9	73.7

* For each set of scores (grammar, vocabulary, etc.) the change over Readings 1, 2, and 3 — $p<.0001$

**GVR is and average of the scores for grammar, vocabulary and cloze

Close examination of these mean scores made it possible to note overall changes in both the values for miscue categories and for the language proficiency test scores. As Table 1 illustrates, the language proficiency means for all subjects increased significantly over time (from Reading 1 to 3) on the scores for each of the test variables, suggesting that the subjects' overall language competence increased over time. Notice especially the increase in the cloze scores (1st reading, 46.5; 2nd, 65.3; 3rd, 74.7) and average scores over all tests (1st reading, 51.4; 2nd, 66.9; 3rd, 73.7). Cloze is generally accepted as a good indicator of overall language proficiency (Oller, 1973; Alderson, 1979) and the average score provides a very general measure of combined language proficiency in a number of areas.

Table 2 lists the significant correlations between the language proficiency scores and miscue frequencies for all readings. In order for a correlation to be significant over all readings, it had to be greater than (+) or (-) 0.305. The significant correlations ($p<.01$) found in the analysis were:

1. Full semantic acceptability correlates positively with GVR, composition, cloze and AVG Scores, while
2. No semantic acceptability has a negative correlation with GVR Composition, cloze, and AVG.

3. Full syntactic acceptability correlates positively with listening, composition, and AVG, while
4. Partial syntactic acceptability shows negative correlation with composition and AVG.

No other significant correlations were found to exist over all three readings.

In order for correlations to be significant for the individual readings and the test scores for those readings, they must be greater than (+) or (-) 0.561. Not surprisingly, since the sample size is much smaller (20 compared to 60), fewer significant correlations emerged. Those that emerged generally matched the correlations found between language proficiency data and overall frequencies for all readings. For example, at each reading, cloze scores showed significant positive correlation ($p<.01$) with full semantic acceptability. There were a few significant correlations which, although they appeared in neither the grand correlation (all readings and all test scores) nor in each of

Table 2. Significant Correlations (Pearson Product Moment)* — Language Proficiency and Miscue Frequencies Values (for all readers)

TEST	MISCUE CATEGORY	CORRELATION
GVR	full semantic acceptability	0.3689
GVR	no semantic acceptability	−0.3142
Listening	full syntactic acceptability	0.3244
Composition	full semantic acceptability	0.3244
Composition	no semantic acceptability	−0.3473
Composition	partial semantic acceptability	−0.3770
Composition	full syntactic acceptability	0.3557
Cloze	full semantic acceptability	0.4426
Cloze	no semantic acceptability	−0.3703
AVG	partial syntactic acceptability	−0.3390
AVG	full syntactic acceptability	0.3429
AVG	full semantic acceptability	0.3152
AVG	no semantic acceptability	−0.3112

*$p<.01$

the individual readings (Sessions 1, 2, and 3), are worthy of note. These correlations appear in Table 3. For Reading 1, there is a significant negative correlation between grammar test scores and full semantic acceptability, and a significant positive correlation between these scores and no semantic acceptability. For Reading 3, scores from the discrete point vocabulary test correlate negatively with full semantic acceptability and positively with partial semantic acceptability.

Table 3. Significant Correlations (Pearson Product)* — Grammar and Vocabulary Test Scores at Readings 1 & 3 and Miscue Frequency Values

TEST		MISCUE CATEGORY	CORRELATION
Reading 1	Grammar	full semantic acceptability	−0.6607
	Grammar	no semantic acceptability	0.6861
Reading 2	Vocabulary	full semantic acceptability	−0.5693
	Vocabulary	partial semantic acceptability	0.5643

*p<.01

The four hypotheses posited earlier concerning the interaction of language proficiency and reading behavior can be examined now in light of the correlation analysis summarized above.

Hypothesis 1.
Increases in reading proficiency, as determined by more efficient reading strategies (see footnote 2), will show a significant, positive correlation with increases in overall language competence.

The hypothesis predicts that as general language proficiency increases, reading behavior will become more efficient, especially in regard to the use of strategies involving semantic cues in oral reading. The correlation analysis partially confirms this hypothesis. Increases in language proficiency, as measured by GVR, composition, cloze, and overall average test scores correlate with increases in frequency of full semantic acceptability of oral reading miscues. Both Clarke (1980) and Cziko (1980) agree that good readers can be characterized by this concern for maintaining semantic acceptability in their reading. The analysis also revealed a significant positive correlation between full syntactic acceptability and scores for composition, listening tests and AVG. Although it is not surprising to find increases in syntactic acceptability over time for L2 readers, good reading has often been defined as the gradual movement away from syntactic and towards semantic information as a way of deriving meaning from a text. Hence these results do not confirm Hypothesis 1.

The hypothesis also predicts that there will be a negative correlation between high graphic and phonemic similarity and increases in language competence; that is, it predicts that readers will rely less heavily on visual cues in reading as they become more proficient in the language. The data do not bear out this part of the hypothesis. No significant correlations, positive or negative, were found between test scores and graphic and phonemic frequencies of miscues. The mixed results for Hypothesis 1 suggest a number of possibilities. The readers of the current study, although they have obviously improved over the course of the research, may not yet be good readers. Hence, their strategies may show a mix of reading behaviors. Another possibility is that the definition of good reader needs to be expanded to include a more active role for the use of graphic and especially syntactic information. It might well be the case, as Clarke points out (personal communication, February 18, 1985), that less reliance on visual and syntactic information in a text is not a necessary condition for good reading. Good readers may attend to various sorts of cues in differing proportions at different times. On the other hand, overreliance on graphic (and perhaps syntactic) cues may well be the cause of poor reading comprehension, since dependence on these cues severely restricts a reader's flexibility in responding to other possible sources of meaning. Finally, oral reading and/or testing may distort the reading behavior of the subjects and give a false picture of actual reading strategies.

Hypothesis 2.
  Poor reading strategies, as indicated by high frequencies of oral reading miscues with no or low semantic and syntactic acceptability, will show a significant, negative correlation with increases in overall language proficiency.

Hypothesis 2 predicts an inverse relationship between increases in language competency and poor reading behavior which is characterized by the production of oral reading errors with no or limited syntactic and semantic acceptability. The data confirm this hypothesis (see Table 2). Notice that every negative correlation involves either "no semantic acceptability" or "partial syntactic acceptability." This suggests, for the readers of the current study, that as general language proficiency (measured by GVR, composition, cloze, and overall test scores) increases, there is less likelihood of the use of poor reading strategies, which result in syntactically and semantically unacceptable oral reading miscues.

Hypothesis 3. and Hypothesis 4.
There will be a significant, positive correlation between increased reading proficiency and holistic measures of language competence. There will be negative or no correlation between increased reading proficiency and discrete point measures of language competence.

Both hypotheses are very generally confirmed by the data, although the former more strongly than the latter. Each of the language proficiency scores in Table 2 which shows a positive correlation with increased reading proficiency (i.e., GVR, Listening, Composition, cloze, and AVG) can be regarded as an integrative or holistic measure of language competence, since these instruments are not meant to test any single component of language in isolation. Those tests which do attempt to isolate and test individual parts of the language (grammar and vocabulary tests), on the other hand, do not show a significant correlation with increases in reading proficiency. For any one reading, they might even show a negative correlation (see Table 3).

The lack of correlation between scores on grammar and vocabulary tests and gains in reading proficiency, and the occasional negative correlation between increases in these test scores and frequency of full semantic acceptability for miscues (see Table 2) is especially interesting as it is precisely these areas that are thought to play a critical role in the development of reading proficiency. As noted above, vocabulary drills and grammar training, particularly at lower proficiency levels, often substitute for actual reading instruction. The assumption that gains in vocabulary and in discrete grammar point will enhance reading proficiency is not substantiated by the results of this investigation.

Summary of Findings

1. Increasing language competence correlates positively with increases in syntactic and semantic acceptability of oral reading miscues (and perhaps with increasingly effective reading strategies).
2. Increasing language competence correlates negatively with high frequencies of no or low syntactic and semantic acceptability.
3. Gains in language competence as measured by holistic tests correlate positively with increasing reading proficiency.
4. Gains on discrete point grammar and vocabulary tests correlate negatively with increasing reading proficiency.

Pedagogical Implications

As the research reaffirms the relationship between general language proficiency and reading performance, we want to insure that reading students have reached a minimal level of competence in the target language. Teachers should not rely on repetition and drilling of grammatical structures to aid students in developing the needed competence. The research clearly suggests that improvements in specific points of language, as seen by increased scores on grammar tests, do not correlate with reading improvement. Rather, the teacher should provide a rich linguistic environment in which readers will be exposed to topically interesting and situationally appropriate language samples. This might be accomplished through the use of tapes, dialogues, and even carefully screened reading material which even low language proficiency readers could follow. The language would be learned, as much as possible, through reading, not as a prerequisite for reading.

The research further indicates that no correlation exists between gains in overall language competence and a reader's ability to reproduce the graphophonemic features of a text. Since an increase in language proficiency seems to enhance the reader's ability to use efficient reading strategies, this finding suggests—as volumes of miscue research has so clearly demonstrated—that close attention to the sounds and letters of the text is an inefficient reading strategy. The author discourages students from adopting a view of reading as faithful reproduction of text words and sounds. In the reading classroom, this would mean no pronunciation drills, no drills of any type that might directly or indirectly encourage students to attempt to improve their reading by closer attention to the print features of the text.

Finally, the lack of correlation (and perhaps negative correlation) found between gains in grammar and vocabulary test, and advances in reading ability implies that if language instruction is to have a positive impact on reading performance, that instruction should be holistic or integrative, rather than discrete-point or skills oriented. Teachers should not adopt materials in the ESL classroom that isolate parts of language—word identification, vocabulary drills, and so forth. Rather, they should provide students with texts which allow them to encounter complete, self-contained stories and articles. Texts of this type allow students, even at beginning levels, to build understanding through the use of a variety of cues, both in the text and from their own experiences as readers and as language users. In addition, tests administered to second language readers at any level should share the features of the texts that are being used; tests should be holistic and integrative, not directed at any one skill but requiring students to use a variety of linguistic and nonlinguistic information in their attempt to understand meaning.

References

Alderson, J. C. (1979). The cloze procedure as a measure of proficiency in English as a foreign language. *TESOL Quarterly, 13,* 219-227.

Alderson, J. C. (1984). Reading in a foreign language: a reading problem or a language problem? In J.C. Alderson & A. H. Urquhart (Eds.), *Handbook of reading research* (pp. 1-24). New York: Longman.

Allington, R. (1984). Oral reading. In P. D. Pearson (Ed.), *Handbook of reading research* (pp. 829-864). New York: Longman.

Carrell, P. L., & Eisterhold, J. C. (1983). Schema theory and ESL reading pedagogy. *TESOL Quarterly, 17*, 553-573.

Clarke, M. A. (1979). Reading in Spanish and English: Evidence from adult ESL students. *Language Learning, 29*, 121-150.

Clarke, M. A. (1980). The short-circuit hypothesis of ESL reading—or when language competence interferes with reading performance. *Modern Language Journal, 64*, 203-209.

Cunningham, J. W., & Caplan, R. (1982, May). Investigating the concurrent validity of miscue analysis as a measure of silent reading. *Reading World*, pp. 299-310.

Cziko, G. A. (1978). Differences in first and second language reading: the use of syntactic, semantic and discourse constraints. *Canadian Modern Language Review, 34*, 473-489.

Cziko, G. A. (1980). Language competence and reading strategies: A comparison of first and second language oral reading errors. *Language Learning, 30*, 101-116.

Devine J. (1984). ESL readers' internalized models of the reading process. J. Handscombe, R. Orem, & B. Taylor (Eds.), *On TESOL '83* (pp. 95-108). Washington, DC: TESOL.

Eskey, D. (1973). A model program for teaching advanced reading to students of English as a second language. *Language Learning, 23*, 169-184.

Goodman, K. S. (1967). Reading: A psycholinguistic guessing game. *Journal of the Reading Specialist, 6*, 126-135.

Goodman, K. S. (1973). Psycholinguistic universals of the reading process. In F. Smith (Ed.) *Psycholinguistics and reading* (pp. 21-29). New York: Holt, Rinehart and Winston.

Hudson, T. (1982). The effects of induced schemata on the "short circuit" in L2 reading: Non-decoding factors in L2 reading performance. *Language Learning, 32*, 1-31.

Leu, D. (1982). Oral reading error analysis: A critical appraisal of research and application. *Reading Research Quarterly, 17*, 420-437.

Oller, J. W. (1973). Cloze tests of second language proficiency and what they measure. *Language Learning, 23*, 105-118.

Weaver, C. (1980). *Psycholinguistics and reading: From process to practice.* Cambridge, MA: Winthrop.

Wilson, M. (1984, May). Developmental reading for adult ESL speakers. Paper presented at the International Reading Association Convention, Atlanta.

Wixson, K. L. (1979). Miscue analysis: A critical review. *Journal of Reading Behavior, 11*, 163-175.

Author's Notes

Thanks to Mark A. Clarke and Andrew D. Cohen for their very useful comments on an earlier draft of this paper.

Footnotes

[1] For a thorough review of relevant literature on this topic as well as suggestions for further research, see Alderson, 1984.

[2] Increased reading proficiency is here operationally defined as the use of more efficient reading strategies, i.e., less reliance on graphic, and to a lesser extent syntactic, cues and increased reliance on semantic cues and on nontextual informa-

tion, that is, higher order schemata.

[3]Readers unfamiliar with miscue analysis are referred to works in bibliography by Goodman (1967-1973) and Weaver (1980).

Comments on Devine

David E. Eskey

University of Southern California

Of Devine's two sets of findings, the second is by far the more interesting. The first simply confirms what most of us who work with second-language readers have known for some time: A positive correlation between general proficiency in a language and the ability to read well in that language exists. Put in the simplest terms, the better you know a language, the better you can read it. There is, of course, some positive value in formally confirming, in a controlled research context, what we think we have learned from experience. At the very least, it allows us to say, depending on our degree of dishonesty, "the research suggests" or "the research shows." Nonetheless, we don't really feel that such research has taught us something that we didn't know.

With respect to the first set of findings, however, two interesting footnotes are in order. One concerns Devine's discovery that her good readers did not move from relying on syntactic cues to relying on semantic cues. Rather, they showed steady improvement in both kinds of processing. The other concerns Devine's related discovery that the readers did not move away from using visual cues but continued to pay close attention to them, as well as to the meaning of the language of the text. What this suggests is that reading *is* an interactive (not a strictly top-down) process in which successful readers continue to make use of cues at all levels, from graphophonic to schematic. Good reading is not a print-free guessing game.

But for those concerned with *teaching* second language reading, Devine's second set of findings is of major interest: the confirmation of her two hypotheses regarding holistic and discrete-point language learning. As many have argued, the words and structures of a language cannot be force-fed to students; more precisely, this force-feeding can only prepare students for discrete-point tests, not for real-world language acts such as reading. Reading must be learned in contexts of communicative use. As Widdowson (1981) noted, acquisition *is* use. In a study of reading proficiency, we unexpectedly encounter strong support for some version of communicative language teaching. The temptation to target particular words and structures for learning, as preparation for doing certain kinds of reading, must be carefully balanced against the need to subordinate all such lists of forms to meaningful classroom activities. Unless the latter condition is met, no real acquisition occurs, at least none that applies to reading or to most other real-world uses of language.

Devine's research strongly supports a recurring paradox: Much of what must be learned cannot be taught. For those concerned with turning theory into practice, designing reading courses geared to that reality will remain a major challenge for some time to come.

References

Widdowson, H. (1981, November). The relationship between teaching and subject matter: Practical implications. Paper presented at American International Education and Training, Inc., San Francisco.

Does Syntactic Rewriting Affect English for Science and Technology (EST) Text Comprehension?

Judith B. Strother

Florida Institute of Technology

Jan M. Ulijn

Eindhoven University of Technology

Does Syntactic Rewriting Affect English for Science and Technology (EST) Text Comprehension?

Authentic texts are often thought to be more difficult to comprehend than simplified ones. One reason for this is the complexity of the syntax in authentic texts. The purpose of this study is to compare differences obtained between scores on a reading comprehension test by university students who read an authentic computer science journal article and those who read a syntactically simplified version of the same article. The test questions were the same for each group. We predicted that the group reading the syntactically simplified test would not have significantly higher scores than those reading authentic texts.

Background

A knowledge of syntax is a required for reading comprehension. According to Nilagupta (1977, p. 585), "The rules of syntax are not just the rules that the writer applies to organize his statments—they are the rules he assumes the receiver knows in order to be able to extract the meaning from statements. For the reader, grammar and syntax are the key to comprehending language."

Aldermon and Alvarez (1978, p. 4) stated "It is clear that grammatical information can convey meaning. Identifying words as nouns, not adverbs, presumably helps one to divide up the sentence and get at the syntax, which helps one to make predictions as to what the sentence might mean." However, the amount of analysis of syntax done by the reader in certain situations may vary considerably, according to such psycholinguists as Hatch (1983) and Ulijn (1984). Both have analyzed linguistic factors which are specific to second language reading comprehension strategies using psycholinguistic models of reading. These models "clearly distinguish several linguistic levels operating in reading: textual, syntactic, morphemic, lexical, graphophonemic or graphemic, which have been experimentally evidenced in reading" (Ulijn, 1980, p. 453). Even though there is interaction among these linguistic factors, there is the need to isolate the individual factors which contribute to problems with reading comprehension.

There have been an increasing number of studies on the characteristics of English for science and technology (EST) (see Trimble, Trimble, & Drobnic, 1978; Ulijn, 1984, 1985). These studies show that there are some syntactic structures that appear with greater frequency in scientific and technical text than they do in text which is written in the common register. It might be assumed then that knowledge of these specific structures would improve a student's reading comprehension level. Foley (1985, p. 28) lists "knowledge of the syntax and lexis associated with a subject area," first in his list of "areas necessary to a successful reader of science and technological type texts." According to Statman (1976) university students become confused when reading professional material in their field because of their inability to recognize or to distinguish between certain grammatical constructions.

Some of these specific syntactic structures are known to cause difficulty in comprehension. For example, Charrow and Charrow (1979) found that subordinate passives, *as to* phrases, and nominalizations caused problems in jury instructions. However, our research partially contradicts some of these findings, for we found that syntactic simplification of the text does not necessarily improve reading comprehension.

Hypothesis

This research took structures that occur with greater frequency in the EST register (Ulijn, 1985) and simplified those structures: passives, nominalizations, and participles. The experiment was conducted to test the validity of the hypothesis that no significant differences would be obtained between scores on a reading comprehension test by university students who read an unsimplified and those who read a syntactically simplified computer science journal article. Differences in scores among the following subgroups were examined: computer science majors and humanities majors whose first language is English; computer science majors whose first language is Dutch or Chinese and whose second language is English; and non-computer science majors who have heterogeneous first languages but whose second language is English.

Method

Subjects

The subjects were from Florida Institute of Technology (FIT) in Melbourne, Florida, USA and Eindhoven University of Technology in the Netherlands, and included both undergraduate students in their third or fourth year and beginning graduate students.

Table 1 shows a summary of subjects and research design by native language, background knowledge of computer science, and language register of the text to be read.

Of the 48 American students from FIT, 24 were computer science majors and 24 were humanities majors with no formal training in computer science.

Table 1. Number and Distribution of Subjects

	E_1		E_2							
	American		Dutch		Chinese		Spanish		Arabic		Other
Language Register: A = authentic B = syntactically simplified	A	B	A	B	A	B	A	B	A	B	A	B
Background Knowledge: Computer Science Majors (experts)	12	12	12	12	11	11	8	7	11	9	15	19
Humanities majors (novices)	12	12										
Mixed Majors (novices in C.S.)												
TOTALS	48		24		22		15		20		34	

The Dutch subjects, who were computer science majors from Eindhoven University, had English as a second or foreign language.

In the US, 71 ESL students with heterogeneous language backgrounds also participated in the study. Twenty-two Chinese students, who had been in the US approximately 9 months, were computer science majors and had TOEFL scores of 550+, or had completed their language requirements at FIT Language Institute. The other 49 ESL students, most of whom had been in the US from 3 to 9 months, represented the following languages: 15 were Spanish-speaking, 20 were Arabic-speaking, and the others spoke Bahasa Malaysian, Danish, Dutch, Farsi, French, German, Greek, Hebrew, Hindi, Icelandic, Indonesian, Italian, Japanese, Korean, Portuguese, Swedish, Telugu, Thai, Turkish, and Urdu. These ESL students had just started the advanced technical reading class in the intensive ESL program at FIT. Their TOEFL scores ranged from 475 to 547.

The Dutch students had a comparable English background: 6 years of English at the secondary school level and considerable exposure to English textbooks during their 3 years of study. Both in the US and in the Netherlands, the level of English knowledge was high intermediate to advanced.

Materials

A computer science article, which had no mathematical formulas or illustrations, was chosen for the test. The article, "Mass Storage Systems and Evolution of Data Center Architecture," came from the July, 1982 issue of *Computer*. Ten one-sentence passages, equally distributed over the entire text, were chosen for rewriting. They contained nominalizations, passives, and participle constructions pertinent to the EST register and mainly functioned to make the agent secondary to the action. These sentences were rewritten in a syntactic form more suitable for a common language (CL) version.

Care was taken not to change the meaning of any sentence. No lexical items or other elements of the original sentences were changed. Therefore, the same content load was maintained. To strengthen the internal validity of the tests, both the revised version of the article and the question set were checked by a computer science professional to ensure that changing the syntax in the text indeed did not change the meaning of the text and that the questions accurately queried information from the article.

The following two sentences from the article are examples of the syntactic simplification from the EST register to a common language register done for this research project.

Authentic text: *Replacement* at a higher system level *is required*; this implies considerable software development to take advantage of these promising device characteristics.

Revised text: The user must *replace* current devices with optical data disks at a higher system level. The programmer must *develop* considerably more software to take advantage of optical data disks.

Authentic text: When such movement is possible under system control, the problem becomes one of *separating* and *clustering* sets of files independently of the physical volumes and *providing* a mechanism to have desired files more readily available.

Revised text: When such movement is possible under system control, the problem is: can the system *separate* and *cluster* sets of files independently of the physical volumes and *provide* a mechanism to have desired files more readily available.

Two types of test booklets were made: Test Booklet A used the authentic article and Test Booklet B used the partly rewritten version. Both were followed by the same ten true-false statements referring in random order to the ten passages that had been rewritten in the text.

Procedure

Subjects were randomly assigned to one of the two test forms. Subjects were asked to record the time spent on reading the text and the time taken to respond to the true-false statements.

Design and Statistical Analysis

Two 2x2 factorial designs (posttest-only control group) were used with the following independent variables (factors) and conditions:

1. Language background:
    (1) native English (American)
    (2) ESL/EFL (Dutch)
2. Background knowledge of students:
    (1) computer science (expert)
    (2) humanities (novice in computer science)
3. Language register of the text:
    (1) authentic version (EST)
    (2) syntactically simplified version

Additional data came from subjects with other language backgrounds. The dependent variables were number of answers correct on the comprehension test and text reading time. The 2x2 design type allowed for chi-square analyses over the comprehension scores and reading times. *T*-tests between two versions of the text were calculated over the comprehension scores and reading times for the additional groups of ESL speakers with different lan-

Results

Table 2. Mean Number of Correct Answers for E_1 Students

	Language Register of Text	
	A	B
Background Knowledge of Students	Authentic Version N = 24	Syntactically Simplified Version N = 24
Computer Science (experts) N = 24	8.25	8.58
Humanities (novices in C.S.) N = 24	7.25	8.17

Maximum score = 10

Tables 2 and 3 show the results of the tests for E1 students. There is no significant effect of language register and background knowledge according to a chi-square analysis ($x^2 = 0.15$) for the American subjects. From that we can conclude that there is no significant difference between the reading comprehension level of versions A and B and between American computer science and humanities majors in the comprehension scores. The same is true for the time they spent in reading both versions of the computer science text in their native languages ($x^2 = 3.57$).

Tables 4 and 5 show the results of the test for ESL students. Analysis of the scores for ESL students shows that there is no significant difference between the comprehension scores for authentic and syntactically simplified versions, neither for the Chinese computer science majors ($t = 1.039$), for the Dutch computer science majors ($t = -1.442$), nor for the non-computer science majors of other non-English language backgrounds: Spanish ($t =

Table 3. Reading Times in Minutes for E_1 Students

	Language Register of Text	
	A	B
Background Knowledge of Students	Authentic Version N = 24	Syntactically Simplified Version N = 24
Computer Science (experts) N = 24	9.5	11.42
Humanities (novices in C.S.) N = 24	10.83	9.25

-1.864), Arabic ($t = -1.777$), and other ($t = -1.143$). The same is true for the time they spent in reading both versions of the computer science text. T-tests showed no significant difference. For the Chinese students, $t = 1.013$; for the Dutch students, $t = 0.257$; for the Spanish speakers, $t = 2.532$; for the Arabic speakers, $t = 1.522$; and for others, $t = 0.410$.

In summary, statistical analysis has shown that there were no significant differences among various groups, whether controlling for language background, background knowledge of the subject to be tested, or the register of the text itself.

Discussion

The conceptual strategy of reading proposed by Ulijn (1981) and demonstrated by French and Dutch subjects reading French instructions to find their way through an imaginary town (Beausite) has been largely confirmed. Both native and nonnative readers of an English computer science text adopt a conceptual strategy aiming at content words and overlook all kinds of syntactic variants that have usually been assumed to be simplifications: nominalizations versus verb phrases, passive versus active constructions and participle constructions versus subordinate clauses. In the experiment, the revisions from a scientific and technical register syntax into a more simplified

Table 4. Mean Number of Correct Answers for ESL Students

		Language Register of Text	
		A	B
Background Knowledge of Students	Non-English Language Background	Authentic Version N = 69	Syntactically Simplified Version N = 70
Computer Science Majors (experts)	Chinese N = 22	8.9	8.4
	Dutch N = 24	9.3	9.7
Non-Computer Science experts	Spanish N = 15	7.1	8.7
	Arabic N = 19	6.4	8.2
	Others N = 34	7.5	7.7

Maximum score = 10

common language syntax affected neither the comprehension scores nor the reading time. Background knowledge of computer science (experts vs. novices) also did not affect the scores or the reading time. The particular language background of the nonnative readers did not affect the results. The syntactic adaptation of the English computer science text did not really help subjects to comprehend better or to read more quickly, neither for the natives (Americans) nor for the nonnatives (Dutch, Chinese, Spanish, Arabic, or other language backgrounds).

However, there are some tendencies, which, while not statistically significant, are striking. Comprehension in all language groups is slightly better with syntactic revisions of the text, for both expert and novices, native and

Table 5. Mean Reading Times for ESL Students

		Language Register of Text	
		A	B
Background Knowledge of Students	Non-English Language Background	Authentic Version N = 69	Syntactically Simplified Version N = 70
Computer Science Majors (experts)	Chinese N = 22	26.3	23.4
	Dutch N = 24	17.3	16.4
Non-Computer Science experts	Spanish N = 15	22.0	14.8
	Arabic N = 19	26.8	21.7
	Others N = 34	19.6	19.3

nonnative readers, with the exception of Chinese computer science majors. They comprehended the original text slightly better than the simplified test. As we find in other reading research literature, lower comprehension scores correlate with longer reading times, with the exception of American and Chinese computer science majors. The Americans took longer to comprehend the simplified text while the Chinese took longer to comprehend the original text. As could be expected, nonnative readers spent more time in processing the text than native readers: The Dutch students took nearly twice as long, and the Chinese and Arabic students took almost three times as long.

However, even with these tendencies, our results support a conceptual strategy used by both native and nonnative readers of EST texts: A thorough syntactic analysis is unnecessary. Syntactic simplification into a more common language register does not really increase readability.

What are the implications for these findings? For authors and publishers, the implications are noteworthy. Ulijn (1984) points out that the way in which people read a text in their native language or a foreign language should have an impact on how the text should be written. In a number of experiments, the conclusion is that what is needed is not syntactic rewriting of professional texts but lexical rewriting to increase readability. Especially for EST students, the lexical area that should be focused on most is the semi-technical vocabulary since that seems to cause the most trouble, mainly as a result of multiple meanings for a single word.

For researchers, the hypothesis of partial parallelism between conceptual and syntactic analysis in reading (Ulijn, 1980, 1984) has been confirmed for English as a native and a second language.

The results are important for classroom teachers to apply. There is the need to help students develop strategies for reading texts with high levels of comprehension. Instead of a focus on syntax, the focus should be on developing skills to obtain the required information from the text and on developing both the technical and subtechnical vocabulary. Students should be guided towards focusing more on concepts and on vocabulary, with syntactic analysis being superficial in most cases. Improving the readability of materials given to students will strengthen their reading comprehension of academic materials.

References

Aldermon, C., & Alverez, G. (1978). *The development of strategies for the assignment of semantic information to unknown lexemes in text*, Mexico City: Autonomous Metropolitan University. (ERIC No. Document Reproduction Services ED 177863).

Charrow, R. P., & Charrow, V. R. (1979). Making legal language understandable: Psycholinguistic study of jury instructions. *Columbia Law Review, 79*, 1306-1374.

Foley, J. A. (1985). Reading skills in science and technology for the L2 student. In J. M. Ulijn & A. K. Pugh (Eds.), *Reading for professional purposes: Methods and materials in teaching languages* (pp. 43-55). Louvain: Acco.

Hatch, E. M. (1983). *Psycholinguistics: A second language perspective*. Rowley, MA: Newbury House.

Miller, S. W. (1982). Mass storage systems and evolution of data center architecture. *Computer*, 16-19.

Nilagupta, S. (1977). The relationship of syntax to readability for ESL students in Thailand. *Journal of Reading, 20*, 585-594.

Statman, S. (1976). Teaching grammar for purpose of comprehension to students of English as a foreign language at university level. (ERIC No. ED 132864).

Trimble, Todd M., Trimble, L., & Drobnic, K. (Eds.). (1978). *English for specific purposes: Science and technology*. Corvallis: Oregon State University, ELI.

Ulijn, J. M. (1980). Foreign language research: Recent trends and future prospects. *Journal of Research in Reading, 3*, 17-37.

Ulijn, J. M. (1981). Conceptual and syntactic strategies in reading a foreign language. In E. Hopkins & R. Grotjahn (Eds.), *Studies in language teaching and language acquisition* (pp. 129-166). Bochum, Federal Republic of Germany: Brockmeyer.
Ulijn, J. M. (1984). Reading for professional purposes: Psycholinguistic evidence in a cross-linguistic perspective. In A. K. Pugh & J. M. Ulijn (Eds.), *Reading for professional purposes: Studies and practices in native and foreign language* (pp. 66-81). London: Heinemann.
Ulijn, J. M. (1985). *The scientific and technical register and its supra-linguistic constants and variants.* Unpublished manuscript.

Authors' Notes

This experiment is the fruit of American-Dutch cooperation between Florida Institute of Technology and Eindhoven University of Technology. The authors are indebted to Dr. Thomas Hand for his help with checking the syntactic rewriting of the text, verifying the questions, and confirming the equivalence of both versions, and to Mr. Jelle Buizer and Mr. Lennard Peeters, technology and communication students, for their experimental and statistical assistance.

Comments on Strother and Ulijn

James Coady

Ohio University

Strother and Ulijn have investigated an important question: Is it worthwhile to rewrite technical material syntactically in order to significantly improve comprehension?

Their answer is *no*. First, I want to discuss their methodology for arriving at this answer and then the original question.

The authentic and rewritten texts were presented to native and nonnative speakers of English who were either computer science or humanities majors. Each of these groups answered comprehension questions on the passages. These answers were then compared statistically in order to find out if there were any differences between the groups. The authors do not tell us what level of statistical significance they expected, only that it was not reached. In future research of this type, it would be best to use an analysis of variance approach in the statistical treatment because it is much more sensitive to such differences and would be more definitive. For example, there is a possible ceiling effect in the data produced by the Dutch computer science majors, that is, they scored 9.3 and 9.7 out of a possible score of 10.0 on the authentic and simplified versions. This probably does not leave enough variation in scores to enable the statistical technique employed by Strother and Ulijn to function properly in this particular area of the data.

The major problem with this type of statistical approach is that it is trying to prove a negative; this is always a difficult task. In other words, they are arguing that they did not find a difference, and so there was no difference. The problem with this assertion is that one could always respond that they did not look carefully enough; an alternate statistical treatment or a different sampling procedure, for example, might find a difference. Hence the suggestion that future research use an analysis of variance treatment.

There is also some question about what the authors actually accomplish in their syntactic simplification. They carefully retain the same lexical items in both texts and change nominalizations, passives, and participle constructions to a more active form. However, in the second example they cite, this procedure would appear to have little effect upon the meaningfulness of the text.

Ulijn's previous research found that readers adopt a conceptual strategy aimed at content words and in the process overlook all kinds of syntactic variants. We are now back to the original question.

In attempting to measure the readability or difficulty of a given text, it has long been known that vocabulary load is the most significant predictor. As Chall points out, "once a vocabulary measure is included in a prediction formula, sentence structure does not add very much to the prediction" (1958, p. 157). It must be kept very clearly in mind that readability formulas are an index or measure of text difficulty, not a causal analysis of why a given text is difficult. For example, Gough (1965), Slobin (1968), and Blount and Johnson (1973) found that active statements are verified more readily and retained better than passive statements. Moreover, Coleman and Blumenfeld (1963) and Rohrman (1968) found that sentences using nominalizations were more difficult to comprehend and recall than those using active verbs.

In general, research has shown that texts which have been made more readable are read in less time with greater reader satisfaction. On the other hand, there is not always improved comprehension or retention. The reasons for mixed results in this regard seem to revolve around the effect of reader motivation, purpose, and background knowledge upon the task. For example, improved readability will have less effect upon a reader's comprehension if the reader already knows a great deal of what a text says before reading it.

In the study under discussion, the native speaker humanities majors did read the simplified version in less time and with higher mean scores (although not significantly so), whereas this was not the case with the native speaker computer science majors.

One is forced to conclude that more research is needed on the important issue that Strother and Ulijn raise. How much of the difficulty of an EST text can be attributed to syntactic variables such as passives, nominalizations, and so forth; do they really lower comprehension significantly? Furthermore, other important variables such as background knowledge and level of motivation will have to be factored into such studies in an appropriate manner.

References

Blount, H. P., & Johnson, R. E. (1973). Grammatical structures and the recall of sentences in prose. *American Educational Research Journal, 10*, 163-168.

Chall, J. S. (1958). *Readability*. Columbus: Ohio State University.

Coleman, E. B., & Blumenfeld, J. P. (1963). Cloze scores of nominalizations and their grammatical transformations using active verbs. *Psychological Reports, 13*, 651-654.

Gough, P. B. (1965). Grammatical transformations and speed of understanding. *Journal of Verbal Learning and Verbal Behavior, 4*, 107-111.

Rohrman, N. L. (1968). The role of syntactic structure in the recall of English nominalizations. *Journal of Verbal Learning and Verbal Behavior, 7*, 904-912.

Slobin, D. I. (1968). Recall of full and truncated passive sentences in connected discourse. *Journal of Verbal Learning and Behavior, 7*, 876-881.

High-Level Reading in the First and in the Foreign Language: Some Comparative Process Data

Gissi Sarig

Everyman's University

High-Level Reading in the First and in the Foreign Language: Some Comparative Process Data

Past research into the issue of the relation between first language (L1) and second/foreign language (L2) reading calls for methodological refinement and for an in-depth qualitative exploration of reading processes in both L1 and L2 (Alderson, 1984). Such exploration is now possible, thanks to recent advances in mentalistic measures methodology for the purpose of researching problem-solving learning tasks (Ericsson & Simon, 1980; Cohen & Hosenfeld, 1983; Cohen, 1984).

This study reports part of a larger research project in the processes of the comprehension of academic texts in Hebrew as a first language and English as a foreign language (Sarig, 1985a). The research project was designed to answer Alderson's call for various methodological improvements and Cohen's recommendation to use mentalistic measures for the elicitation of process data.

The research as a whole sought to answer the following questions: What is the relative contribution of L1 reading strategies[1] and L2 language proficiency to L2 reading? Are reading processes in L1 and in L2 related, and if so, in what way? The first question was studied quantitatively (N = 130), and the second question was studied qualitatively (N = 10). This report deals with the qualitative section of the research.

Reading comprehension in general is viewed in this research as resulting from the four-way intersection between reader-text-task-activity characteristics (see Brown, 1982; Brown, Campione, & Day, 1981). The success of this interaction depends on the availability and quality of content and strategic schemata and on the reader's degree of expertise in transferring these schemata to new problem-solving situations (see Brown, 1982; Brown, Campione, & Day, 1981).

The process of reading in a foreign language is viewed in this research as the interlingual transfer of reading skills from the readers' metamodel (native) language (see de Beaugrande, 1984; Baten & Cornu, 1984). Success in L2 reading is viewed as dependent on the same conditions as in L1. An additional condition, however, is the ability to make skillful changes which derive from the new linguistic and cultural reading environment. The L2 reading is therefore viewed as a process of transfer-in-learning taking place in an interlingual context.

Since the aim of this study was to make a comparative exploration of L1 and L2 reading processes, the following questions were asked:

1. What reading processes characterize the performance of main ideas analysis and overall message synthesis tasks in Hebrew as a first language and English as a foreign language?
2. Do reading processes in the first language transfer to the foreign language?

Subjects

The subjects were ten female high school seniors, from ages 17 to 18, averaging roughly 8 years of formal English as a foreign language study on a 4 to 5 hour weekly basis. They had received no formal or direct training in reading comprehension as a separate discipline in Hebrew (L1). However, they had already been intensively exposed indirectly to at least 8 years of academic reading material in various content areas. In English (L2) the situation was the reverse. The subjects received formal, basic, but unsystematic training in reading comprehension in EFL, but were exposed to a very limited amount of academic reading material.

The sample consisted of subjects with low, intermediate, and high English proficiency levels, as determined by teacher evaluations and an English proficiency test, consisting of several lexical and sentential substitution tasks: translation into L1, synonym production in context, syntactic rephrasing, and free paraphrase.

Procedures

Materials

Text readability level is viewed here as a product of the interaction of a variety of reader-based, text-based and task-based variables (Mann, 1983; Baten & Cornu, 1984). A multivariate text comprehensibility assessment instrument was developed (Sarig, 1985a) because classical readability evaluation measures, including cloze, fail to account for such complexity. The instrument consisted of (a) a discourse cloze (Levenston, Nir & Blum-Kulka, 1984); (b) a set of evaluation scales for the assessment of pragmatic, textual, and linguistic variables; and (c) a comparative rhetorical analysis component. The discourse cloze was taken by a group of subjects parallel to the experimental subjects. The evaluation was done by two groups of seven expert readers from various professional backgrounds (see Huckin & Olsen, 1984). The comparative rhetorical analysis was done by the researcher.

Pairs of texts of equivalent difficulty levels were chosen on the basis of the discourse-cloze results. The results of the two other assessment components were used to select the best pairs to suit the subjects. The target challenge level was I + 1 (Cohen, 1983). During the pre-experimental training stage, final decisions were made as to which particular pair of texts would best suit each subject individually. It was hoped that this process would ensure that the subjects work with texts as close as possible to the I + 1 level.

The Pre-Experimental Training Stage

The pre-experimental training stage consisted of two demonstration and training units carried out separately for two different purposes: (a) to ensure that all subjects understood the experimental tasks, and (b) to ensure elicitation of mentalistic data which would be reliable and valid (Ericsson & Simon, 1980; Cavalcanti, 1983; Mann, 1983; Cohen, 1984).

To achieve the first aim, the experimenter explained the task, handing out printed instructions with short model answers based on a short, easy text. The subjects were given answers to clarify various questions they asked. No practice of the reading tasks was offered at any stage. To achieve the second aim, subjects received a written preparation sheet describing the purpose and the process of the experiment, and providing a list of vivid examples of the kind of data desired. At a later stage, the experimenter demonstrated think-aloud and introspection data production to the subjects. Finally, the subjects practiced verbalizing with the supervision and support of the experimenter.

The Tasks

Reading is viewed in this research as a problem-solving process. It was, therefore, important to set the experiment within an authentic problem-solving context. The tasks assigned in this study were: (a) main ideas analysis and (b) synthesis of overall message.

The first task (main idea analysis) consisted of two subtasks: identification of main propositions, and elimination of peripheral and background information. The second task (synthesis of overall message) consisted of these same subtasks, plus two interrelated additional subtasks: identification of macrosynthesis schema underlying the text (e.g., a paradox, a comparison of opposing views); and the identification of the microschemata components comprising the macroschema (e.g., statement + counter statement + contradiction + settling statement).

These subtasks were later used as a basis for task performance evaluation. At the preparation stage the subjects were told only what the two main tasks were, with no explicit, metacognitive explanation as to the nature of the various subskills. However, the task performance demonstration by the experimenter included the performance of all subtasks. This ensured that the subjects were given a good idea of what they were expected to do without formal training.

HIGH-LEVEL READING: SOME COMPARATIVE PROCESS DATA

The Experiment

The experiment took place in an informal, supportive setting, outside the school. The subjects were told that there was no time limit for the completion of the task. The duration of the experiment varied considerably with regard to different subjects. Some finished the tasks in both languages in one 140 minute session, including a 20 minute break. Others needed two 80 to 140 minute sessions to finish the tasks in both languages. In addition, some subjects' task performance duration changed from session to session. Five subjects performed the tasks first in Hebrew and then in English. The other five did them in reverse order.

As a general rule, the experimenter tried to disappear from the scene by keeping silent and not reacting in any way to the subjects' performance. This enabled the experimenter to take detailed notes describing the subjects' nonverbal reactions to the task, such as gestures, facial expressions, and actions related to writing, marking, underlining, and so forth. These observations served later as an aid to the interpretation of the recorded verbal data.

However, when the subject became nervous, hesitated, or lapsed into silence longer than a few seconds, the experimenter intervened. The intervention was of two main types: (a) Encouragement and support were given in the case of growing nervousness; for example, "You're doing just fine, please go on"; "That was good, why don't you go on?"; and (b) Indirect encouragement to continue was given in the case of prolonged silence; for example, "What are you thinking now?" or "Is anything bothering you?" These questions referred only to information available from the short-term memory (see Ericsson & Simon, 1980; Cohen, 1984).

The Data Analysis Model

The unit of analysis, *the reading move*, referred to each separate action the reader took while processing the text: for example, highlighting a word in the text, increasing redundancy through syntactic simplification paraphrase, identification of macro-frame of the text, identification of incompatibility of a newly-deciphered idea with a formerly identified one, and so forth. As can be seen from these four examples, some moves were overt and directly demonstrated in reading activity, while others were covert and had to be inferred; for instance, the covert move, identification of macro-frame of the test was inferred from the utterance, "It's something to do with women's lib." Similarly, "this doesn't make sense" was interpreted as identification of incompatibility of a newly identified idea with a formerly identified one.

The data were analysed along three dimensions. First, reading moves were located and interpreted. They were classified into categories representing their core function. Second, each move was evaluated as to its effect on the overall success in performing the reading tasks. Thus, all moves were divided into two categories: (a) comprehension promoting moves and (b) comprehension deterring moves. Finally, the data were classified according to stages in the problem-solving process. The three stages were: (a) the proposition identification stage, (b) the identification of main proposition (idea) stage, and (c) the synthesis of overall message stage.

Findings and Discussion

Reading Moves Types and Their Function in the Task Performance Process.

Four types of reading moves were identified in the data: (a) technical-aid moves, (b) clarification and simplification moves, (c) coherence-detecting moves, and (c) monitoring moves.

All moves that showed the reader using a technical aid to facilitate text processing were identified as *technical-aid moves*. These included strategies such as skimming, scanning, skipping, marking and writing key elements in the text, differential marking for different purposes, margin paragraph summary, using glossary, and so forth. The data showed that technical-aid strategies promoted comprehension under the following conditions: (a) varied repetoire (including a variety of technical-aid moves); (b) reader's appropriate conception of the task and reader's choice of techniques appropriate to task and task performance plan; and (c) effective activation of appropriate technique the reader had selected.

All moves which displayed the reader's intention to clarify and/or simplify utterances in the text were classified as *clarification and simplification moves*. These included various types of utterance substitutions, such as raising redundancy level by means of syntactic simplification, decoding meanings of word and groups of words in context by means of synonyms and/or circumlocutions, ideational simplification by means of proposition analysis, rhetoric function paraphrase ("Here he gives us an example . . . warns us not to forget that . . . " etc.), indirect question paraphrase and implication paraphrase ("He says here that up till now there was no chance this would happen. This means that now there's a chance . . . "), and various other types of paraphrase. The data show that effective comprehension-promoting clarification and simplification moves depend on the following two conditions: (a) effective lexical, morphological, syntactic and rhetorical recognition of utterances in context, and (b) effective sizing of unit to be simplified. Of all move types, this seemed to depend more than others on the readers' language proficiency.

All moves which displayed the reader's intention to produce coherence from the text, whether by means of textual cues or extratextual cues, were identified as *coherence-detecting moves*. These included identification of the macroframe of the text, effective use of prior extratextual content schemata (knowledge of the world), identification of people in the text and views or actions attributed to them, identification of key information in the text, reliance on textual schemata norms for the purpose of prediction about text development ("I'm sure he will now give an example, so I might as well skip it and go on . . . " etc.), cumulative decoding of text meaning, use of overt cohesive cues, identification of overall textual schemata ("Now I get it: he first shows what's wrong. Then he says what should be done. Finally he says exactly how."), relying on summarizing units identified in the text, relying on identified overt purpose of text, use of macroproposition as starting point in the synthesis task, identification of text focus ("this is actually the most important thing here"), reproduction of logical development of text, and other such similar coherence-detecting moves. The data show that effective processing of discourse coherence depends on the following conditions:

1. The existence of rhetorical-textual schemata in the reader's data base and knowledge of overt and covert coherence patterns;
2. Awareness of the existence of the rhetorical functions of texts;
3. The existence of relevant and correct content schemata in the reader's data base;
4. The retrieval of complete, correct, and contextually relevant content schemata from the reader's data base; and
5. The ability to identify ideas/views in the text even when they stand in contrast to the reader's own views/outlook/norms.

"This means he recommends speculation, utopia and rebellion. Funny. So unrealistic and unpatriotic. But this is what he recommends, no doubt about it." (correct interpretation) vs. "He criticizes them because they want something unrealistic-utopia." (incorrect interpretation).

Moves displaying active monitoring of text processing, whether metacognitively conscious or not, were identified as *monitoring moves*. It is quite obvious that no moves of any type can be comprehension promoting without effective monitoring. Moves classified in this category, however, are characterized as direct moves intended to actively monitor text processing. These include conscious change of planning and carrying out the tasks; controlled and conscious hold moves ("I'll get back to this later, after I read the example"); deserting a hopeless utterance ("I'll just leave that be. I won't be able to make head or tails of it anyway, so I don't want to lose any more time on it"); flexibility of reading rate; identification of misunderstanding and incompatibility of formerly interpreted material with newly interpreted material ("What's going on here?"); mistake correction; ongoing self-evaluation; self-directed dialogue; controlled skipping; slowing down and using singsong intonation to facilitate comprehension; repeated reading of same decoding unit and repeated skimming or scanning. The data show that success in monitoring comprehension depends on the following conditions: (a) the constant awareness of the task to be performed, (b) the awareness of the need to control consistency of task performance, (c) the ability to identify failure in comprehension, (d) the ability to recruit various resources for the purpose of error correction, (e) the ability to evaluate correctly one's chances of handling a difficulty, (f) the ability to control decoding efforts, and (g) the ability to tolerate fuzzy comprehension when necessary.

Table 1 presents a crosslingual distribution of move types functioning across the three task stages.

Table 1. Contribution of Moves Types To Success/Failure In Reading Task Across The Task Stages In Hebrew and English

		Technical Aids		Clarification & Simplification		Coherence Detecting		Monitoring	
		CPMs	CDMs	CPMs	CDMs	CPMs	CDMs	CPMs	CDMs
Hebrew	%	22%	29%	18%	12%	34%	36%	26%	22%
	N	15	17	12	7	23	21	18	13
English	%	22%	28%	18%	12%	34%	37%	26%	23%
	N	15	16	12	7	23	21	18	18

CPMs = Comprehension Promoting Moves
CDMs = Comprehension Deterring Moves

The data show that move type functioning across task performance stages is almost identical in both languages. Coherence-detecting moves contribute most (approximately 1/3) to both overall success and failure. In contrast to this, the most language dependent move type— clarification and simplification— contributes to success least of all (approximately 1/5 to overall success and 1/10 to overall failure) in both L1 and L2.

In both L1 and L2 the contribution of monitoring and technical-aid moves to success, as compared to their contribution to failure, is graded somewhat differently. Whereas monitoring moves come second in contribution to success, they come only third in contribution to failure. Similarly, while technical-aid moves come second in contribution to failure, they come only third in contribution to success. However, the coherence-detecting move (the most important move) and the clarification and simplification move (the least important move) are graded identically in both languages with regard to both success and failure.

HIGH-LEVEL READING: SOME COMPARATIVE PROCESS DATA

Table 2. Distribution of Contribution of Move Types to Success/Failure Within Each Move Type

		Technical Aids	Clarification & Simplification	Coherence Detecting	Monitoring
			HEBREW		
Total Move	N	32	19	44	31
CPMs	%	47%	63%	52%	58%
CDMs	%	53%	37%	48%	42%
			ENGLISH		
Total Move	N	31	19	44	31
CPMs	%	48%	63%	52%	58%
CDMs	%	52%	37%	48%	42%

Table 2 presents a crosslingual within-move distribution of the contribution of each move type to overall success and failure in task performance. The data show that all four move types function in both languages in almost identical ways. The move type which functions more negatively than positively in comparison to all other move types is the technical-aid move type. The majority of moves of this type are comprehension-deterring. This means that relatively speaking, when the function of each move type is considered separately, the readers benefit least of all from their repertoire of technical-aid moves. The reader's task performance process is then characterized by more comprehension-deterring technical moves than by comprehension-promoting technical-aid moves.

In contrast to this, the readers use clarification and simplification moves more to their advantage. The proportion between comprehension-promoting and deterring moves within this group shows that readers clarify and simplify utterances significantly more successfully than unsuccessfully.

The majority of the two other move types—monitoring moves and coherence-detecting moves—is also more comprehension-promoting than deterring, though the proportion between their contribution to success and failure seems to be more balanced.

Transfer of Reading Moves: The Group Perspective

To look into the transfer question, the Pearson product moment correlation between frequencies of the same moves in both languages was computed across the ten subjects. The findings are presented in Table 3.

Table 3. Zero-Order Correlations Between Frequency of Moves in Hebrew and in English

Stage	Correlation Between Comprehension-promoting Moves in L1 and L2	Correlation Between Comprehension-deterring Moves in L1 and L2
Across the Three Stages	.77 (n = 66)	.75 (n = 60)
Content Proposition Analysis	.54 (n = 34)	.74 (n = 22)
Main Ideas Selection	.84 (n = 20)	.83 (n = 22)
Overall Message Synthesis	.84 (n = 12)	.91 (n = 16)

(All correlations are significant at the .001 level.)

These findings both corroborate and refine the findings summarized in Table 1. They show that, except for success in the proposition decoding stage where there is only a moderate correlation (r = .54 p<.001) between Hebrew and English, there is a considerable relation between task performance processes in both languages (r = > .74 <.91 p = .001).

The first stage of the task performance (proposition identification) is more dependent on language proficiency than the other two stages (Sarig, 1985a). Therefore, this finding is not surprising. It should be noted, however, that the processes in the first stage differ noticeably in both languages only in as much as comprehension-promoting moves are concerned. The correlation between comprehension-deterring moves at this same stage is quite high (r = .75 p <.001). This means that in the more language-specific stage in task performance the processes in L1 and L2 differ only with regard to comprehension-promoting moves. The same wrong moves seem to characterize processes in both languages to quite a high degree. It also seems that the more global the moves are, the more substantial the correlation is between the processes in both languages, especially when failure is concerned. This is not surprising, because it seems logical that local moves are more language specific than global ones.

The data seem to suggest that readers tackle high level reading tasks in both languages in a similar manner. The same factors explain success and failure to almost the same extent. In addition, there appears to be a considerable relation between the frequency of comprehension-promoting and deterring moves. One may conclude, then, that reading processes do transfer crosslingually, as far as main ideas analysis and overall message synthesis tasks in an academic text are concerned.

Individual Reading Style and Transfer of Reading Skills: Focus on the Reader

In this section of the paper, data relating to reading processes of individual readers will be presented. Individual reading style was examined from the following perspective: (a) uniqueness of personal reading strategies and (b) number and variety of reading strategy repertoire.[2]

Table 4 presents data relating to degree of uniqueness of moves. The moves were classified according to four degrees of uniqueness, depending on the number of users and frequency of use: (a) maximally unique/used by only four or fewer subjects with different intensity (i.e., frequency); (b) unique/used by only four or fewer subjects with similar rates of intensity; and (c) moderately unique/used by more than four subjects with different intensity; and (d) not unique/used by more than four subjects with a similar rate of intensity.

Table 4. Strategy Uniqueness Degree

	Degree 1 (Maximally Unique Strategies)	Degree 2 (Unique Strategies)	Degree 3 (Moderately Unique Strategies)	Degree (Lacking Uniqueness Strategies)
%	22%	38%	27%	13% (T=100%)
N	29	51	37	17 (T=134)

The data presented in Table 4 show that reading is a highly individual process. Only 13% of the moves observed show no degree of uniqueness; that is, they are used by most readers with a similar degree of intensity. All other moves show uniqueness of various degrees: 38% (N=51) moves are unique in the sense that four or fewer subjects used them with similar intensity, 27% (N=37) are unique in the sense that more than four subjects used them, but with different intensity, and 22% (N=29) were maximally unique, that is, were used by only 4 subjects or fewer in a different intensity rate.

These data lead to one of the major findings in this study: 87% of the reading moves observed are unique. This means that most of the reading comprehension process consists of the readers' use of a unique, personal combination of moves which characterizes them as individuals. This finding is also in line with the classical concept of reading processes as schemata-based. The various moves observed have to do with a variety of schemata types, such as content schemata, textual conherence schemata and strategic schemata. This finding, then, is in line with an interactive-integrative view of the reading process (e.g., Rumelhart, 1980; de Beaugrande, 1984; Baten & Cornu, 1984).

Another dimension of the reading profile studied was the variety of the reading move repertoire (i.e., the number of different moves in the personal combination of moves) in the personal repertoire. The two columns of Table 5 present data concerning this aspect of the personal reading profile. The intrasubject degree of variance of number of moves used is rather low (7 in Hebrew and 5 in English). This means that readers do not differ as greatly in the number of moves they use to solve a reading problem (i.e., the variety level of their personal strategy combination) as they do in the particular strategy selection which characterize them (i.e., the personal reading move combination). Moreover, variety level of the repertoire does not seem to discriminate between high/low task scorers.

These findings seem to challenge the traditional dichotomy between the good and the poor reader (see Hosenfeld, 1979). This dichotomy is often used in the context of various prescriptions meant to encourage good reading behavior (see Clarke, 1979). The personal move combination data show that readers use different good reading strategies (that is, combinations of moves)

Table 5. Number of Moves in Individual Reading Repertoire

	HEBREW	ENGLISH
GHILLA	64	55
IRIS	63	50
HADAR	72	63
LIOR	58	54
YIFAAT	58	50
ADI	56	47
HADASS	59	56
YOSEFFA	54	49
TALI	71	57
ORNA	60	53
Mean:	62	53
S.D.:	7	5

for the same purposes. Similarly, they seem to be original in the type of poor strategies that make them fail. Moreover, readers may use a majority of comprehension promoting moves and still fail as a result of a few wrong moves or even a single wrong move. This does not turn them into poor readers. The same is true of readers who make more comprehension-deterring than comprehension-promoting moves and still perform the task successfully, thanks to even one smart move which outweighs the other comprehension-deterring ones.

Summary and Conclusions

The following answers to the research questions present themselves. First, four move types were identified as underlying main idea identification and overall message synthesis tasks in Hebrew as a first language and English as a foreign language to almost the same extent.

A most important feature of the nature of the reading process in both languages was found to be its high degree of individuality. One of the main dimensions of the personal reading style was the personal reading strategy (the individual combination of reading moves). Readers were shown to be characterized by their own reading assets and reading drawbacks. These changed from reader to reader. Therefore, the findings in this study do not seem to corroborate the classical dichotomy between good and poor reading, with the implication it carries for material development and reading process tests. Success in reading was shown to be a result of the quality of the reader's unique combination of moves rather than the occurrence of certain moves or lack of others.

Second, the same processes were found to underlie task performance processes in both L1 and L2. The same reading strategy types accounted for success and failure in both languages to almost the same extent. In addition to this, reading was found to be of a highly individual nature to almost the same degree in both languages. It can be concluded, then, that reading processes from the first languages do appear to transfer to the foreign language.

It seems necessary to further corroborate the findings of this research on a larger scale. Replications of design and methodology, with different text type, task level, age and languages are also needed. If future research does corroborate these findings, they may carry implications for the teaching and testing of reading skills. Such possible implications will concern increasing the individual orientation of text processing curriculum design and of material and test development.

References

Alderson, J. C. (1984). Reading in a foreign language: A reading problem or a language problem? In J. C. Alderson & A. H. Urquart (Eds.), *Reading in a Foreign Language* (pp. 1-27) London: Longman.

Baten, L. (1981). *Text comprehension: The parameters of difficulty in narrative and expository prose texts: A re-definition of readability.* Unpublished doctoral dissertation, University of Illinois.

Baten, L., & Cornu, A. M. (1984). Reading strategies for LSP texts: A theoretical outline on the basis of text function, with practical application. In A. K. Pugh & J. M. Ulijn, *Reading for professional purposes: Studies and practices in native and foreign languages* (pp. 190-202). London: Heinneman.

de Beaugrande, R. (1984). Reading skills for foreign languages: a Processing approach. In A. K. Pugh & J. M. Ulijn, *Reading for professional purposes: Studies and practices in native and foreign languages* (pp. 4-27). London: Heinneman.

Brown, A. L. (1982). Learning and development: The problems of compatability, access and induction. *Human Development, 25,* 89-115.

Brown, A. L., Campione, J. C., & Day, J. D. (1981). Learning to learn: On training students to learn from texts. *Educational Researcher, 10,* 14-21.

Cavalcanti, M. (1983). Using the unorthodox, unmeasurable verbal protocol technique: Qualitative data in foreign language reading research. In Katamba, F. (Ed.), *Proceedings of the University of Lancaster colloquium on problems, method and theory in applied linguistics* (pp. 72-86). Lancaster: Department of Linguistics and Modern English, University of Lancaster.

Clarke, M. E. (1979). Reading in Spanish and English: Evidence from adult ESL students. *Language Learning, 19,* 121-147.

Cohen, A. D. (1983). Studying SL learner strategies: How do we get the information? *Applied Linguistics, 5,* 101-112.

Cohen, A. D. (1984). The use of mentalistic measures in determining LSP problems. In A. K. Pugh & J. M. Ulijn (Eds.), *Reading for professional purposes: Studies and practices in native and foreign languages* (pp. 177-190). London: Heinneman.

Cohen, A. D., & Hosenfeld, C. (1983). Some uses of mentalistic data in SL research. *Language Learning, 31,* 285-313.

Douglas, D. (1981). An exploratory study in bilingual reading proficiency. In S. Huddleson (Ed.), *Papers in applied linguistics and literacy: Series 1. Learning to read in different languages* (pp. 93-101). Washington, DC: Center for Applied Linguistics.

Ericsson, K. A., & Simon, H. A. (1980). Verbal reports as data. *Psychological Review, 87,* 215-252.

Haynes, M. (1983). Patterns and perils in second language reading. In J. Handscombe, R. Orem, & B. P. Taylor (Eds.), *On TESOL '83* (pp. 163-177). Washington, DC: TESOL.

Hosenfeld, C. (1979). Cindy: A learner in today's foreign language classroom. In N. C. Brown (Ed.), *The learner in today's environment* (pp. 53-75). Montpellier, VT: Capital City.

Huckin, T. N., & Olsen, L.A. (1984). On the use of informants in LSP discourse analysis. In A. K. Pugh & J. M. Ulijn (Eds.), *Reading for professional purposes: Studies and practices in native and foreign languages* (pp. 120-130). London: Heinneman.

Levenston, E., Nir, R., & Blum-Kulka, S. (1984). Discourse analysis and the testing of reading comprehension by cloze techniques. In A. K. Pugh & J. M. Ulijn (Eds.), *Reading for professional purposes: Studies and practices in native and foreign languages* (pp. 202-213). London: Heinneman.

Mann, S. (1981). Problems in reading and how they may be solved by the reader. Unpublished manuscript, University of Lancaster, Department of Educational Research.

Mann, S. (1983). Verbal reports as data: A focus on introspection. In F. Katamba (Ed.), *Proceedings of the University of Lancaster Colloquium on Problems, Method and Theory in Applied Linguistics* (pp. 87-109). Lancaster: Department of Linguistics and Modern English, University of Lancaster.

Rumelhart, D.E. (1980). Schemata: The building blocks of cognition. In R. J. Spiro, B. L. Bruce, & W. F. Brewer (Eds.), *Theoretical issues in reading comprehension* (pp. 33-58). Hillsdale, NJ: Earlbaum Associates.

Sarig, G. (1985a). Comprehension of academic texts in the mother tongue and in a foreign language. Final Draft of Ph.D. Dissertation, Hebrew University of Jerusalem.

Sarig, G. (1985b, May). Can we be fair to reading comprehension test-takers? Paper presented at the Sixth International ACROLT Convention, Kriyat-Anavim.

Sarig, G. (1985c, July). Compensation strategies in L2 reading. Paper presented at the Jerusalem Conference on TEFL-TESOL, Jerusalem.

Sarig, G. (1985d, October). The individual reading profile. Paper presented at the Conference of the Israeli Association for Applied Linguistics, Tel Aviv.

Smith, S. (1979). Strategies, language transfer and the simulation of the second language learner's mental operations. *Language Learning, 29,* 345-361.

Author's Note

This paper is based on a section of a doctoral dissertation, written under the supervision of Professor Andrew D. Cohen, School of Education, Hebrew University of Jerusalem. I am indebted to Professor Cohen for his endless efforts to guide and support me, professionally as well as morally.

Footnotes

[1] Smith, S. (1979) says that as long as we don't have a clear psycholinguistic explanation as to what "a strategy" is, we can at best regard it as a problem solving process. It seems necessary, then, to clearly and consistently distinguish between *the reading problem* to be solved (or *reading objective to achieve*) and *the process* of solving it. In this study the objectives were the tasks. Each step the reader took to achieve them is interchangeably referred to as a "move" and/or a "strategy."

[2] Other dimensions of the personal reading profile studied in this research are: (a) Reading Intensity, (b) Origin of Success, (3) Individual Transfer patterns. Findings related to these dimensions showed that transfer intensity is not related to either success in L2 reading or to L2 proficiency level. Differences in L1 and L2 reading intensity level showed that L2 readers compensate for deficiency in L2 proficiency by increasing the intensity of their global nonlanguage-specific moves (Sarig, 1985a; 1985c; 1985d).

Comments on Sarig

Fraida Dubin

University of Southern California

No longer scorned as an unsuitable research tool, introspective and mentalistic studies are now respectable in psycholinguistic studies of the processes which take place in language learning. The approach seems particularly valuable in studying the nature of reading comprehension since it gets at what is going on quite literally beneath the surface of the investigator's scope of observation. Beginning with Hosenfeld's pioneering work in foreign language reading in which she developed think-aloud procedures (1977), the method has now been utilized by other researchers, notably Cohen and Hosenfeld (1983), and defended by Cohen (1984).

Sarig's paper contributes to the use of think-aloud research methodology in addition to posing questions about the relationship of first and second language strategies. Sarig's subjects read Hebrew natively while English is their foreign language. Her results show that their Hebrew reading processes did transfer to their English reading.

Along the way, there is an interesting fall-out from her investigation which may have more long-term implications than the findings themselves. It comes about through her need to classify the data derived from her subjects' self-reports. In order to quantify the results, she sets up four general types of responses (moves) made by the subjects: (a) technical aid, (b) clarification and simplification, (c) coherence detection, and (d) active monitoring of one's own text processing. The significance of Sarig's paper lies as much with this first attempt to classify learners' strategies as it does with the results which she obtained from the study as a whole.

Textbook writers, particularly, have tended to group together all kinds of activities or exercises which give learners guided practice in getting meaning from a text. For example, skimming, scanning, marking and writing in a text are mixed with organizational matters, such as identifying text types or macroframes (Sarig's term). They all tend to appear without any clear-cut motivation for including them. At the same time, reading techniques, such as adjusting one's rate to the nature of the text, slowing-down, and skipping redundant material, are apt to be treated in the directions for reader-learners or in the introduction for their teachers. Such matters infrequently receive attention in practice sections.

Sarig's classification can go a long way toward giving materials preparers a more systematic base upon which to create meaningful activities. Making some slight adjustments to Sarig's four categories, materials preparers need to consider the differences among four areas in which strategic intervention in the reading process can take place: (a) applying skills to the text, (b) dealing with the nature of the text in terms of its organizational, grammatical and lexical features, (c) activating the reader's subject content or background knowledge in order for comprehension to take place, and (d) helping learners become aware of their own reading processes through self-monitoring.

Sarig's formal results indicate that her subjects did carry over strategies from L1 into L2 reading. One wonders, however, how Sarig managed to synthesize the tangle of variables which she had wisely brought in at the beginning—her view of reading comprehension as the "4-way interaction between reader-text-task-activity characteristics." Considering the text alone raises some thorny questions. As Sarig's subjects were female high school seniors, ages 17-18, what were the academic texts they read in the study? They could not have been professional papers or journal articles; the subjects did not have enough specialized background knowledge. What academic material can high school seniors handle even in their first language beyond a textbook which makes use of secondary sources or possibly a popular magazine article? Is it accurate to label such texts as academic reading? In fact, is all academic reading the same? Clearly it is not. In order to evaluate the real significance of Sarig's findings, it would be helpful to know more about the actual texts which the subjects read.

Sarig also points out that her results cast a shadow on the distinction between poor and good readers which she claims has been posited by reading researchers. However, this finding is probably no more than a terminological one, at best. In fact, in Hosenfeld's (1984) more recent work in which she further describes think-aloud research in L2 reading, she uses the terms successful and unsuccessful reader, in relation to particular texts, as opposed to the more general good and poor. Though this terminology may be more accurate, it is still essentially evaluative. But Sarig's point is well taken when she says that an individual's reading "moves" are unique, and that there is no easy formula for making the right moves. Better L2 reading instruction may come about through emphasizing a repertoire of reading strategies, along with providing the necessary background knowledge of both subject matter and textual content for understanding a particular text.

References

Cohen, A. D. (1984). The use of mentalistic measures in determining LSP problems. In A. K. Pugh & J. M. Ulijn (Eds.), *Reading for professional purposes: Studies and practices in native and foreign languages* (pp. 177-190). London: Heinneman.

Cohen, A. D., & Hosenfeld, C. (1983). Some uses of mentalistic data in SL research. *Language Learning, 31,* 285-313.

Hosenfeld, C. (1977). A preliminary investigation of the reading strategies of successful and non successful language learners. *System, 5,* 110-123.

Hosenfeld, C. (1984). Case studies of ninth grade readers. In J. C. Alderson & A. H. Urquhart (Eds.), *Reading in a foreign language* (pp. 231-249). London: Longman.

Cognitive Strategy Transfer in
Second Language Reading

Keiko Koda

Ohio University

Cognitive Strategy Transfer in Second Language Reading

Background

1. Orthography and Cognition

The relationship between language and cognition is one of the most critical issues in socio- and psycholinguistic research. Whether orthographic systems have any significant cognitive consequences has been investigated over the past 30 years. One line of research has been conducted by sociologists and historians who have demonstrated that the evolution of orthographic systems directly influenced social development, especially in the West (Goody, 1968; Goody & Watt, 1963; Olson, 1975, 1977; Gelb, 1963). Gelb (1963) points out that through history the development of writing was a major factor in the formation of civilizations. Goody (1968) argues that the extension of speech in time and space has affected all aspects of human social activities. Olson (1975, 1977), moreover, claims that the decontextualization of written texts, which is essential to the development of philosophical and scientific thought, could not have been attained without the prerequisite invention of alphabetic systems. These systems helped reduce one-to-one correspondence either between symbols and meaning, or symbols and sounds. Olson further argues that a one-to-one correspondence in prealphabetic systems necessarily restricted their explanatory function to context-bound materials.

Even more striking evidence on the effects of orthography on cognition has been provided by Scribner and Cole (1981). In their widely cited study, they explored the effects of literacy on the cognitive development of an African tribe, the Vai. The researchers administered a series of cognitive tasks to four groups of Vai adults: English literates, Arabic literates, Vai literates, and an illiterate group. They found consistent patterns of differences in performance on different cognitive tasks among the three literate groups, which correlated with the literacy background of each group. The Vai subjects, whether they were literate in English, Arabic, or Vai, performed well on particular tasks which required cognitive operations similar to the script they usually read. Based on their findings, Scribner and Cole claimed that orthography exerts a significant cognitive influence on readers, and that the skills and strategies developed through literacy acquisition are transferred to performance of nonliteracy activities posing similar task requirements.

2. Orthographic Systems and Reading Process

Three major orthographic systems are presently used in written language. In logography, one grapheme generally represents the meaning of one whole word or morpheme. Figure 1 provides examples from Japanese logography. All characters have the same pronunciation; obviously these characters having the same pronunciations

Figure 1. Examples of Japanese logography, Kanji. (Shown are characters with the same pronunciation /sa/)

左	差	作	査
left	difference	to make	to examine
砂	詐	鎖	唆
sand	to cheat	chain	to suggest

do not exhibit common visual features. The logography represents a word's meaning rather than its sound. Learning to read is relatively simple when there is only a handful of words to be coded. However, in the case of an entire spoken language, the logography requires readers to learn as many signs as there are words and morphemes. For example, in Japanese, which uses both logographic symbols and syllables, children are required to learn 996 Kanji (Chinese characters) during the 6 years of elementary school, as well as an additional 949 characters during the 3 years of high school (Japanese Ministry of Education, 1982).

A second system is the syllabary wherein each sign represents a syllable. Since languages usually have fewer syllables than morphemes, a syllabary can represent a spoken language with a smaller number of signs. Another Japanese example can be used since Japanese employs syllabaries as well as Kanji. Each of the Japanese syllabaries (Hiragana and Katakana) consists of 46 basic letters, and two kinds of diacritic marks, which can be added to 25 of the basic letters to represent voiced syllables. A total number of symbols is only 76 for each type of Kana. Examples of Japanese syllabaries are also included in Figure 2.

Figure 2. Examples of Japanese syllabaries.

	Hiragana	Katakana	Pronounciation
Basic letters	は	ハ	ha
	ひ	ヒ	hi
	ふ	フ	fu
	へ	ヘ	he
	ほ	ホ	ho
With Diacritic "	ば	バ	ba
	び	ビ	bi
	ぶ	ブ	bu
	べ	ベ	be
	ぼ	ボ	bo
With Diacritic °	ぱ	パ	pa
	ぴ	ピ	pi
	ぷ	プ	pu
	ぺ	ペ	pe
	ぽ	ポ	po

The third system of orthography is the alphabet in which the unit of representation is the single sound unit of the language, the phoneme. By minimizing one-to-one correspondence between signs and meanings, or signs and phonetic elements, the alphabet reduces the complexity and ambiguity of writing. Consequently, the invention of the alphabetic principle, which made both reading and writing easier, democratized literacy, making it accessible to a wider public (Olson, 1975, 1977; Gelb, 1963).

Given the varying forms of representation in each orthographic system, it can be speculated that the perception of print should differ from one orthographic system to another. Similarly, different cognitive strategies must be involved in the word recognition process for each orthographic system. By definition, word recognition refers to the retrieval process of sound and meaning from the visual configuration of each lexical item. Three elements, therefore, are involved in the process: visual configuration, speech code (i.e., sound used in speech), and meaning. Presumably, the degree to which the speech code is reflected in the visual configuration (hereafter called phonological recodability) is one of the crucial factors in determining the underlying cognitive strategies used for word recognition. In Figure 3, diagrammed models illustrating the word recognition processes for different orthographic systems are presented.

In phonologically shallow or highly decodable orthographies, such as two of the Japanese syllabaries and Serbo-Croatian, visual configuration, speech code, and meaning are lineally related. As the flow-chart in Figure 3 indicates, phonological recoding in such orthographies is essential. Turvey, Feldman, and Lukatela (1984) performed a study to investigate word recognition strategies used by mature Serbo-Croatian readers. The results demonstrate that the strategies used by skilled Serbo-Croatian readers in accessing lexicon involve an analysis of phonological components.

In contrast, in the word recognition process for meaning-based orthographies shown in the far left diagram in Figure 3, speech code and meaning are associated separately, as well as independently, from the visual configuration.

Studies of word recognition process among Chinese readers consistently demonstrate that logographic readers have a direct access to meaning from the visual configuration of a character and can consequently read without going through a phonological recoding process (e.g., Rozin, Poritsky, & Sotsky, 1971; Liberman, Shankweiler, Liberman, Fowler, & Fischer, 1977; Trenman, Baron, & Luk, 1981). Trenman et al. (1981) found that in a silent reading task, English readers had a longer reaction time and made more errors in judging homophone sentences than did Chinese readers reading Chinese. The researchers contend that more phonological recoding occurs in sound-base scripts than in meaning-base scripts.

More striking evidence of variant processing in sound-base versus meaning-base orthographies is available in studies conducted with Japanese subjects reading both syllabic and logographic scripts appearing in the same sentences concurrently. Saito (1981), for example, found that Kana (a Japanese syllabary) is superior to Kanji (Chinese orthographic writing) in facilitating access to the phonemic code. Kanji, on the other hand, affords more rapid

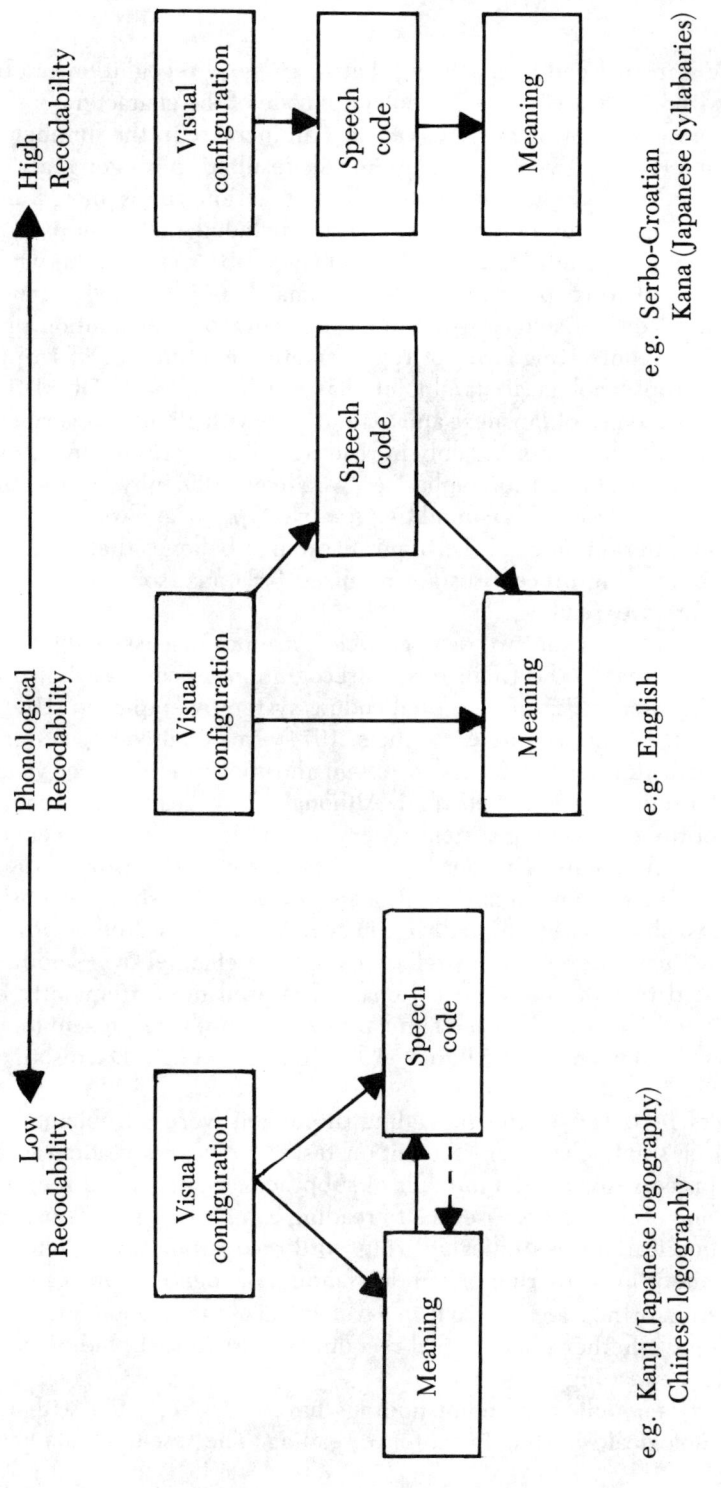

Figure 3. Word recognition process in different orthographic systems.

access to the semantic code, suggesting that Kanji word recognition can be performed without retrieving the phonological code of the character.

Furthermore, Nomura (1981) observed that an increase in the number of letters in Kana (syllabic) word recognition task resulted in longer reaction times compared to only minor variations in reaction times in a Kanji (logographic) word recognition task. Nomura concluded that Kana is processed letter by letter, implying that it is processed by sound units, while Kanji is processed word by word, indicating that it is processed through meaning units. Nomura suggests that differences in word recognition processes reflect the contrasting forms or representation in each type of script.

From a neuropsychological standpoint, Sasanuma (1974a, 1974b, 1975, 1984) studied two types of Japanese aphasiacs, those with a Kana impairment (i.e., aphasiacs who have trouble only in reading syllabic writing) and those with a Kanji impairment (i.e., aphasiacs who have difficulty in reading logographic writing). Sasanuma found that the two types of aphasiac patients had lesions in different areas of the brain. Sasanuma believes that different information processing procedures are required for Kana (sound-base) and Kanji (meaning-base) reading.

English lies between the two orthographic extremes discussed above. It has been argued that in the English word recognition process, as shown in the middle diagram in Figure 3, a dual-coding system is employed (Huey, 1908; Coltheart, 1978; LaBerge & Samuels, 1974). In a dual-coding system, readers use two different channels to obtain the meaning: a direct visual channel and a sound mediated channel. Although there has been a general acceptance of the dual-coding system theory, controversy remains over the way the system functions. Two conceptualizations have been proposed: (a) the two channels complement one another and are activated simultaneously; and (b) the two channels are mutually exclusive. A number of studies, investigating individual differences in preference for one channel over another, have concluded that the direct visual channel is used more frequently by mature or skilled readers and when familiar or easy stimuli are present (e.g., Smith, 1971; Stanovich, 1982; Baron, 1977; Olson, Kliegl, Davdison, & Foltz, 1985).

The results reviewed in the preceding discussion were all obtained in single-word or single-character recognition tasks. However, reading is an integrative process involving a number of subprocesses, and word recognition is only one of the factors essential to reading comprehension. Thus, the theoretical implications of studies utilizing word recognition tasks alone are of limited benefit in furthering our understanding of cognitive processes in reading different orthographies. To gain a true grasp of the phenomenon, we must determine whether phonological recoding occurs in text reading or at least in sentence reading.

Interestingly enough, conflicting findings have been reported with respect to phonological recoding in sentence reading. The research data have been a matter of dispute for the past 25 years. Earlier studies in the 1960s and 1970s consistently reported that phonological recoding is necessary in word recognition (e.g., Levy, 1971; Sperling, 1960; Conrad, 1964). More recent studies, however, have provided evidence which denies the necessity of phonological recoding (Baron, 1973, 1977; Kleiman, 1975). Kleiman (1975) contends that phonological recoding occurs after lexical access, facilitating the temporary storage of words in short-term memory which is necessary in syntactic processing for sentence comprehension.

As a number of short-term memory (STM) studies (Erickson, Mattingly, & Turvey, 1972; Baddeley, 1966; Cimbalo & Laughery, 1967) have demonstrated, acoustic encoding is preferable to visual encoding for the information register in short-term memory. The most recent STM studies done with native speakers of Chinese yield strong evidence supporting the dominance of acoustic encoding regardless of orthographic differences (Yik, 1978; Mou & Anderson, 1981). If acoustic encoding is indeed favored even by readers of meaning-based scripts, such as the Chinese, it can be hypothesized that sentence comprehension in meaning-based scripts also requires phonological recoding. To test this hypothesis, Tzeng, Hung, Cotton, and Wang (1979) conducted two experiments with Chinese subjects. The researchers investigated the effect of phonological interference on the process of word recognition and on sentence comprehension by employing a shadowing task. They found that phonological interference does not affect lexical access, but it has a significantly negative effect on the sentence comprehension process. Tzeng and his associates concluded that phonological recoding does play an important role in reading a logographic script beyond lexical access.

Based on the previous research findings, it seems reasonable to conjecture that phonological recoding of lexical items is vital in reading sentences and texts, whether written in sound-based script or meaning-based script. The studies of the word recognition process mentioned above have limited implications for our understanding of the long-lasting effects of orthographic systems on cognitive strategies in reading. Since the studies were done primarily with a first language (L1) population, the differences between readers of meaning-based and sound-based orthographies could be explained as task-specific rather than orthography-specific effects. In order to obtain convincing evidence of orthographic consequences for reading, we must determine whether strategy differences among L1 readers using different orthographic systems still exist when they must use an alternative orthographic system. If writing systems have significant effects on reading strategies, readers should use the strategies acquired in L1 when reading a second language (L2). Therefore, strategy transfer should be observable in L2 reading.

A number of studies on second language acquisition have reported that the transfer of various linguistic and metalinguistic elements, such as pronunciation (e.g., Tarone, 1980; Broselow, 1983), communicative strategies (e.g., Olshtain, 1983; Scarcella, 1983), and morphosyntactic systems (e.g.,

Hakuta, 1976; Gundel & Tarone, 1983) is present in L2 learners' linguistic production in both oral and written contexts. There has not been corresponding support for the transfer of cognitive skills in the comprehension process.

To summarize, experimental psychologists have suggested that readers of meaning-based and sound-based orthographies develop different word recognition strategies in their first language because of the different nature of representation in each type of orthography. However recent STM studies have demonstrated that phonological recoding is necessary for text comprehension regardless of orthographic backgrounds of the readers. It can be concluded then that the chief difference between readers from differing orthographic backgrounds will be in the strategies used for obtaining an acoustic code for lexical items (hereafter referred to as lexical sounds). Specifically, readers of sound-based orthographies will tend to obtain lexical sounds by direct analysis of phonetic elements whereas readers of meaning-based orthographies will tend to obtain lexical sounds in indirect ways, such as memory search and association. It is hypothesized that strategies developed in L1 reading are transferred to L2 reading and that readers of meaning-based orthographies reading sound-based scripts in a second language will not obtain lexical sounds through phonetic analysis as extensively as readers with sound-based orthographic backgrounds. As a result, phonological inaccessibility will not have as much negative impact on logographical readers as on sound-based readers.

Phonological accessibility is important in the reading process of native English speakers (see Cunningham & Cunningham, 1978; Rubenstein, Lewis, & Rubenstein, 1971; Kleiman, 1975; Baron, 1977). The present study investigated the consequences of phonological inaccessibility on logographic (meaning-based) readers reading a second language written in sound-based scripts.

To test the claim that this inaccessibility will not have the same negative impact on logographic readers reading in a sound-based orthography as it will on sound-based readers reading the same text, the method used in the Cunningham and Cunningham (1978) study was replicated. In the original study, an experiment was conducted to test the print-to-meaning hypothesis. This hypothesis proposes that in silent reading, readers (native speakers of English) process a text directly from print to meaning without going through an intermediate stage of phonological recoding. The researchers constructed a reading task in which the accessibility of the phonological code was controlled. Sixteen graduate students in reading education and 41 5th and 6th graders served as subjects. Both groups were divided into two subgroups, and each subgroup read a passage containing either a set of pronounceable or unpronounceable words.

Test Materials

Six pictures of tropical fish were prepared. Six pronounceable names were typed on 3x5 index cards. Each name contained six letters and two syllables. Only three different initial letters were used, and two words were constructed with each, to prevent the subjects from discriminating on the basis of the first letter alone. The unpronounceable names were constructed by altering the positions of the second and third letters and the fifth and sixth letters of each pronounceable name (Appendix A). Since construction of unpronounceable words inevitably entails orthographic illegality, it was anticipated that two factors — unpronounceability and orthographic illegality — were confounded. In order to minimize the effect of the undesirable second factor, the subjects were asked to learn the six fish names by associating them with pictures prior to the actual experiment.

Imaginary characteristics of the six fish are described in a passage of approximately 450 words (Appendix B). Two passages were constructed — one with pronounceable and one with unpronounceable fish names.

Procedure

The test was given to each subject individually. The subjects were first given the written names of the fish together with the pictures. The pictures were then spread across a table with the appropriate name cards for each fish. The subjects were asked to study the fish names until they felt confident that they could associate the names with the pictures. When the subjects indicated that they had learned the names, they were asked to match the names with the pictures. The matching practice was continued until the subjects could correctly match the names and pictures in two consecutive trials.

When the introductory session was completed, the related reading passage was given to the subjects. They were informed that comprehension questions would be asked afterward. Although reading time was measured, there was no time limit; therefore, they could spend as much time reading as they wished.

Once the subjects completed the passage, the pictures were again spread out, and the subjects were asked to point to the fish which had a particular characteristic described in the text. Next, the name cards were spread out, and the subjects were asked to perform the same task using names rather than pictures.

Results

Cunningham and Cunningham analyzed their results using a 2-factor MANOVA with treatment condition (pronounceable vs. unpronounceable) and age as independent variables, and reading time, name comprehension scores, and picture comprehension scores as dependent variables. The researchers found that main effects (age and treatment condition) were both significant for reading time and name comprehension scores but no significance was found for the third dependent variable, picture comprehension scores (see Table 1). Based on their findings, Cunningham and Cunningham argue that an intermediate stage of phonological recoding takes a significant role even in silent reading process. They speculated that phonological code is used not to retrieve the meaning, but to register what was comprehended into short-term memory. They hypothesized that "fluent readers proceed from print to meaning to sound to memory" (1978, p. 120). See Table 1, following page.

These data obtained from Cunningham and Cunningham's study were compared with results of the present replication involving native speakers of Japanese who learned English as a foreign language in Japan.

Method

Subjects

Twenty-six Japanese university students who came to the US for the summer of 1984 to study English participated in the experiment. They were enrolled in an intensive English program at the University of Illinois. For most of the students, the trip was their first visit to an English-speaking country. Three of the students had been outside Japan for longer than 1 year during childhood, and one of these had lived in the US for 2 years between the ages of 3 and 5. However, no significant differences were found between the reading performance of this group of three students and the rest of the population.

Procedures

The same reading passage and the fish names, both pronounceable and unpronounceable, devised by Cunningham and Cunningham, were used in the present study. The experiment was also conducted by following the procedures used in their original study. Since the subjects of the present study were all second language learners, they were encouraged to ask about the meaning if they could not discover it from the context. Only three subjects asked for the meaning of one or two words during the trials.

In addition to the original experiment tasks, a debriefing interview was conducted to obtain more information about strategies used in performing the tasks. When the subjects finished the two comprehension tasks, both the pictures and the names were displayed. The subjects were asked to describe

Table 1. Results from Cunningham and Cunningham's Study (1978)

	Graduate Students				Elementary Students		
	Time in Seconds	Comprehension Picture	Comprehension Name		Time in Seconds	Comprehension Picture	Comprehension Name
Pronounceable	115.4	5.1	4.3		134.1	1.9	2.6
Unpronounceable	136.7	2.9	2.7		159.3	1.9	1.7

Note: Maximum score of comprehension tasks = 6.

how they learned the names of the fish in the first matching session, and how they recalled these names while reading the passage. The testing and the debriefing interview was carried out in Japanese.

Results

The results were analyzed using a 1-factor MANOVA with treatment condition as an independent variable, and reading time, name comprehension, and picture comprehension as dependent variables. Since the multivariate F for treatment condition was significant ($p < .04$), univariate f's for the three dependent variables were examined subsequently. There was a significant main effect for reading time $AF (1.24) = 7.41$, $p < .01$, but no significance was found for either comprehension scores ($p > .05$) (see Table 2). Subjects in the unpronounceable group read the passage in significantly less time than did subjects in the pronounceable group. This sharply contrasts the results of Cunningham and Cunningham's study conducted with native English speakers.

Table 2. Reading Time and Performance of Comprehension Tasks of Japanese Students

	Treatment Condition		
	Pronounceable	Unpronounceable	F
Reading Time in Seconds	576.6	413.5	7.41*
Comprehension Scores Pictures	5.3	4.6	1.36
Comprehension Scores Names	5.1	4.6	1.26

n = 13 for each condition group.

*$p < .01$.

Note. Maximum score of comprehension tasks = 6.

The results of the self-monitoring report with respect to the strategies used in performing the tasks are presented in Table 3. The most common strategy used by the Japanese students was *renaming*.

Table 3. Strategies Used for Learning Fish Names

	Renaming			Using Original Names	
	Use Familiar word	Use two letters	Use first syllable	For all six fish	For some fish
Pronounceable	3	2	4	2	2
Unpronounceable	6	7	0	0	0

Three methods for renaming were primarily used. In the first method, the students converted the original names into familiar words. For example, the original name *mintex* and its unpronounceable counterpart, *mnitxe* were often converted into *mint, mix,* or *tax*. Then, the second name was associated with physical characteristics of each fish.

The second method was less complex. It involved a simple association between one or two letters used in the original names and the physical characteristics of each fish. For example, an association was made between two *f*s in *doffit* and stripes on the fish body. Thus, when the students saw the striped fish, they associated it with *ff* instead of the original name *doffit*.

The third method was to use only the first syllable consisting of three letters as a name of each fish. For example, *min* for *mintex*, or *dof* for *doffit*. This third method was observed only among the students in the pronounceable group.

Four students in the pronounceable group reported using names in their original form. These students, presumably, obtained lexical sounds of the fish names through grapheme-phoneme recording. Several other students in the pronounceable group combined the strategies of renaming and phonological recoding.

Discussion

It was predicted that, in the case of Japanese students, phonological inaccessibility would not have any negative effects on their reading process. Therefore, significant differences would not occur either in reading time or comprehension task performance between the pronounceable and unpronounceable groups.

As expected, there were no significant differences in comprehension between the two groups. A significant difference, however, was found in reading time. As reported earlier, the unpronounceable group spent much less time reading the passage. This contrasts sharply with the results from Cunningham and Cunningham's study done with native speakers of English which found that phonological inaccessibility has a significantly negative effect on reading performance.

The conflicting results found between the two studies do not necessarily indicate that native speakers of English are more acoustically oriented and Japanese readers are more visually oriented in their reading processes. The self-monitor reports indicate that all of the Japanese students obtained the sound of each fish name in one way or another, which is consistent with the previous finding suggesting that phonological code is necessary for text reading regardless of orthographic background.

The contrastive effects of phonological inaccessibility among Japanese and American readers, therefore, could be attributed to the different strategies used by each group of subjects to obtain lexical sounds. Thus, the results of the study support the primary hypothesis noted earlier: Reading strategies specific to L1 orthography are transferred to L2 reading involving a different orthography. More specifically, phonological recoding is not a common strategy among Japanese readers in reading Japanese. Other strategies, such as association, are more typically used to obtain lexical sounds in their L1 reading. Therefore, when they read English as a second language, they will not obtain lexical sounds through phonetic analysis as extensively as native speakers.

Since the hypothesis of the present study is based upon obtaining a null finding, the results are not, statistically speaking, definitive enough to allow a claim of orthographic effect on reading strategies. However, it seems reasonable to conclude that the findings of the present study have established a theoretical basis for subsequent research. Further investigation should be conducted to explore the relationship between orthography and reading strategies.

Lastly, in order to obtain a clear distinction between Japanese and American readers, the study used subjects who were minimally exposed to spoken English. However, even among beginning level learners, it was observed that those who were more familiar with English, such as an English major, tended to use the decoding strategy more often than others. Although the study was not designed to examine the effects of English proficiency on strategy transfer, a second hypothesis is proposed for future investigations:

> Transfer phenomena are more apparent among beginning L2 learners, especially those who learn the second language in a context where the language is not spoken. As learners improve in their L2 proficiency, especially oral proficiency, their strategies will progressively approximate those most commonly used by native speakers of the target language.

L2 proficiency effects could be profitably investigated either longitudinally or cross-sectionally.

References

Baddeley, A. D. (1966). Short term memory for word sequences as a function of acoustic, semantic, and formal similarity. *Quarterly Journal of Experimental Psychology, 18,* 362-365.
Baron, J. (1973). Phonemic stage not necessary for reading. *Quarterly Journal of Experimental Psychology, 25,* 241-246.
Baron, J. (1977). Mechanisms for pronouncing printed words: Use and acquisition. In D. LaBerge, & S. J. Samuels (Eds.), *Basic process of reading: Perception and comprehension,* (pp. 175-216). Hillsdale, NJ: Lawrence Erlbaum Associates.
Broselow, E. (1983). Nonobvious transfer: On predicting epenthesis errors. In S. M. Gass, & L. Selinker (Eds.), *Language transfer in language learning* (pp. 191-200). Rowley, MA: Newbury House.
Cimbalo, R. S., & Laughery, K. B. (1967). Short term memory: Effects of auditory and visual similarity. *Psychonomic Science, 8,* 57-58.
Coltheart, M. (1978). Lexical access in simple reading task. In G. Underwood (Ed.), *Strategies of information processing.* (pp. 151-216). New York: Academic Press.
Conrad, R. (1964). Acoustic confusion in immediate memory. *British Journal of Psychology, 55,* 75-84.
Cunningham, P. M., & Cunningham, J. W. (1978). Investigating the "print to meaning" hypothesis. In P. D. Pearson, & J. Hansen (Eds.), *Reading: Disciplined inquiry in process and practice* (pp. 116-120). (27th Yearbook of the National Reading Conference). Clemson, SC: The National Reading Conference.
Erickson, D., Mattingly, I. G., & Turvey, M. T. (1972). Phonetic coding of Kanji. *Journal of the Acoustic Society of America, 52,* 133.
Gelb, I. J. (1963). *A study of writing.* Chicago: University of Chicago.
Goody, J. (1968). Introduction. In J. Goody (Ed.) *Literacy in traditional society* Cambridge: Cambridge University.
Goody, J., & Watt, I. (1963). The consequence of literacy. *Comparative studies in society and history, 1,* 5, 304-345.
Gundel, J. K., & Tarone, E. E. (1983). Language transfer and the acquisition of pronominal anaphora. In S. M. Gass, & L. Selinker (Eds.), *Language transfer in language learning* (pp. 281-296). Rowley, MA: Newbury.
Hakuta, K. (1976). A case study of a Japanese child learning English as a second language. *Language Learning, 26,* 321-351.
Huey, E. B. (1908). *The psychology and pedagogy of reading.* Cambridge, MA: Massachusetts Institute of Technology.

Kleiman, G. M. (1975). Speech recording in reading. *Journal of Verbal Learning and Verbal Behavior, 14,* 323-340.

LaBerge, D., & Samuels, S. J. (1974). Toward a theory of automatic information processing in reading. *Cognitive Psychology, 6,* 293-323.

Levy, B. A. (1971). Role of articulation in auditory and visual short term memory. *Journal of Verbal Learning and Verbal Behavior, 10,* 123-132.

Liberman, I. Y., Shankweiler, D., Liberman, A. M., Fowler, C., & Fischer, F. W. (1977). Phonetic segmentation and recoding in the beginning reader. In A.S. Reber & D. L. Scarborough (Eds.), *Toward a psychology of reading* (pp. 207-225). Hillsdale, NJ: Lawrence Erlbaum Associates.

Japanese Ministry of Education. (1982). *Minimal essentials of Language Arts Curruculum in Secondary School.* Tokyo: Tokyo Shoseki.

Mou, L. C., & Anderson, N. S. (1981). Graphemic and phonemic codings of Chinese characters in short-term retention. *Bulletin of the Psychonomic Society, 17,* 255-258.

Nomura, Y. (1981). The information proceeding of Kanji, Kana script: The effects of data-driven and conceptually-driven processing on reading. *The Japanese Journal of Psychology, 51,* 327-334.

Olshtain, E. (1983). Sociocultural competence and language transfer: The case of apology. In S. M. Gass, & L. Selinker (Eds.), *Language transfer in language learning* (pp. 232-249). Rowley, MA: Newbury.

Olson, D. R. (1975). [Review of *Toward a literary society*]. *Proceedings of the National Academy of Education, 2,* 109-178.

Olson, D. R. (1977). From utterance to text: The bias of language in speech and writing. *Harvard Educational Review, 47,* 257-281.

Olson, R. K., Kliegl, R., Davidson, B. J., & Foltz, G. (1985). Individual and developmental differences in reading disability. In G. E. MacKinnon & T. G. Walker (Eds.), *Reading research: Advances in theory and practice, Vol. 4.* Orlando, FL: Academic Press.

Rozin, P., Poritsky, S., & Sotsky, R. (1971). American children with reading problems can easily learn to read English represented by Chinese characters. *Science, 171,* 1264-1267.

Rubenstein, H., Lewis, S. S., & Rubenstein, M. A. (1971). Evidence for phonemic recording in visual word recognition. *Journal of Verbal Learning and Verbal Behavior, 10,* 647-657.

Saito, H. (1981). The use of graphemic and phonemic encoding in reading Kanji and Kana. *The Japanese Journal of Psychology, 52,* 266-273.

Sasanuma, S. (1974a). Kanji vs. Kana processing in alexia with transient agraphia: A case report. *Cortex, 10,* 89-97.

Sasanuma, S. (1974b). Impairment of written language in Japanese aphasics: Kana vs. Kanji processing. *Journal of Chinese Linguistics, 2,* 141-157.

Sasanuma, S. (1975). Kana and Kanji processing in Japanese aphasics. *Brain and Language, 2,* 369-383.

Sasanuma, S. (1984). Can surface dyslexia occur in Japanese? In L. Henderson (Ed.), *Orthographies and reading: Perspectives from cognitive psychology, neuropsychology, and linguistics* (pp. 43-56). Hillsdale, NJ: Lawrence Erlbaum Associates.

Scarcella, R.C. (1983). Discourse accent in second language performance. In S. M. Gass & L. Selinker (Eds.), *Language transfer in language learning* (pp. 306-326). Rowley, MA: Newbury.

Scribner, S., & Cole, M. (1981). *The psychology of literacy.* Cambridge, MA: Harvard University.

Smith, F. (1971). *Understanding reading: A psycholinguistic analysis of reading and learning to read.* New York: Holt, Rinehart & Winston.

Sperling, G. (1960). The information available in brief visual presentation. *Psychological Monographs, 74.* (11, Whole No. 498).

Stanovich, K. E. (1982). Word recognition skill and reading ability. In M. H. Singer (Ed.), *Competent reader, disabled reader: Research and application* F (pp. 81-102). Hillsdale, NJ: Lawrence Erlbaum Associates.

Tarone, E. (1980). Some influences of syllable structure of interlanguage phonology. *International Review of Applied Linguistics, 18,* 139-152.

Trenman, R. A., Baron, J., & Luk, K. (1981). Speech recognition in silent reading: A comparison of Chinese and English. *Journal of Chinese Linguistics, 9,* 116-125.

Turvey, M. T., Feldman, L. B., & Lukatela, G. (1984). The Serbo-Croatian orthography constrains the reader to a phonologically analytic strategy. In L. Henders (Ed.), *Orthographies and reading: Perspectives from cognitive psychology, neuropsychology, and linguistics* (pp. 81-89). Hillsdale, NJ: Lawrence Erlbaum Associates.

Tzeng, O. L. J., Hung, D. L., Cotton, B., & Wang, W. S. Y. (1979). Visual lateralization effect in reading Chinese characters. *Nature, 282,* 499-501.

Yik, W. F. (1978). The effect of visual and acoustic similarity on short-term memory for Chinese words. *Quarterly Journal of Experimental Psychology, 30,* 487-494.

Appendix A

Fish Names

Pronounceable Names	Unpronounceable Names
doffit	dfofti
dulmet	dlumte
mintex	mnitxe
mastib	msatbi
pontud	pnotdu
pemtad	pmetda

Appendix B

Fish Passage

There are six fish which could easily be called the "Six Wonders of the Sea World." These wonderous fish are the mintex (mnitxe), the doffit (dfofti), the pontud (pnotdu), the dulmet (dlumte), the pemtad (pmetda), and the mastib (msatbi).

The mintex (mnitxe), for example, is the fastest fish in the world. Sometimes it has been timed swimming as fast as 40 miles per hour. In a race with a mintex (mnitxe), any other fish would lose. Mintexes (Mnitxes) race each other sometimes as if they were sea racehorses!

The doffit's (dfofti's) claim to fame is just the opposite of the mintex (mnitxe). The doffit (dfofti) is the slowest fish in the world. It has been known to remain in the same place in the water for hours. The doffit (dfofti) doesn't have to worry, though, about not being able to run away from its enemy. The doffit (dfofti) tastes so bad that no other fish will try to eat it.

The pontud (pnotdu) is a famous fish because of the way its body lights up when it falls in love with another pontud (pnotdu). Scientists have tried to figure out how to make flashlights which work on the same chemical that the pontud (pnotdu) has, but they have not succeeded. It is a beautiful sight to see two pontuds (pnotdus), swimming along blinking at each other.

The dulmut (dlumte) is not an unusual fish because it is fast or slow or lights up, but because of how delicious it is to eat. Dulmet (Dlumte) meat sells for $25 per pound in the store where you can find it. Kings and Queens have long considered dulmet (dlumte) a royal dish. Dulmet (Dlumte) is so good that some people eat it raw!

The pemtad (pmetda) is the world's most dangerous fish because it has a poisonous bite. Pemtad (Pmetda) poison is more deadly than rattlesnake venom and there is no antidote for it. Pemtad (Pmetda) fishing is against the law in some countries because of its poisonous bite.

Finally, there is the mastib (msatbi) fish. The mastib (msatbi) fish is so unusual because there is nothing it would rather do than be caught by a fisherman. No bait is necessary to capture a mastib (msatbi). They run straight toward a hook or net. Needless to say there aren't many mastibs (msatbis) left!

Now whether it's the speedy mintex (mnitxe), the slowpoke doffit (dfofti), the flashy pontud (pnotdu), the delicious dulmet (dlumte), the poisonous pemtad (pmetda) or the easy-to-catch mastib (msatbi), you'll have to admit that here are some pretty fishy fish!

Comments on Koda

William Grabe

Northern Arizona University

Keiko Koda's paper elicits a variety of responses. First, as an essentially information processing approach to second language reading research, it ties in well with recent research efforts to develop an information processing model for second language acquisition (e.g., Chaudron, 1984; McLaughlin, Rossman, & McLeod, 1983). Second language research is at present a fragmented field, as second language acquisition research, second language reading research, and second language writing research all seem to be drifting along separate paths. It is, therefore, encouraging to see Koda contributing to a small but growing common ground among different research subdisciplines in second language acquisition.

Second, the central issue in her study, cognitive strategy transfer, is significant for anyone interested in reading theory and second language reading development. This issue is especially important in light of the somewhat simplistic assumption in ESL reading that reading abilities are the same from language to language, and that students must then, by logical necessity, transfer such abilities (c.f., Hudelson, 1981; Tzeng & Hung, 1981; Henderson, 1984).

Third, any research examining cognitive strategy transfer is ambitious. Koda investigates an immensely tangled research area and, to her credit, has provided us with a provocative research study. Koda's review of the literature is extensive and informative. The sources referred to are current and in line with recent reading theory (e.g., Harris & Sipay, 1985; Pearson, 1984; Taylor & Taylor, 1983). The study itself appears to be carefully done and clearly described. Perhaps it is because Koda's study is so clear that I am able to find a number of points where I would like to take issue.

The major question addressed by Koda is whether or not Japanese ESL students are as affected by unpronounceable naming as English-speaking students are. Koda argues that the Japanese students differ significantly from their English counterparts, and provides evidence that the students transferred a strategy from their Japanese reading experience which is not used by the English readers. In order to support this analysis a number of assumptions have been made by Koda, assumptions that need to be explored to weigh both the strengths and weaknesses of the study.

Assumption 1: Reading is essentially controlled by a simultaneous dual processing system.

This assumption is generally a good one to make. My only hesitancy with this view is the implication that there must be only two general processing strategies involved in reading. In much recent theory a basic dichotomy is found between perceptual processing (bottom-up, data driven) and cognitive processing (top-down, concept driven) (c.f., Taylor & Taylor, 1983). This distinction is a good one, and one that is particularly useful to experimental concerns (e.g., Johnston & Hale, 1984). This dichotomy, however, seems to be an oversimplification from a theoretical perspective. Once a parallel processing model is adopted, there is no particularly strong reason to assume only two processes control all the subskills that are indicated in such approaches to reading (c.f., McClelland & Rumelhart, 1981; Monsell, 1984).

Assumption 2: There are language specific reading strategies that are influenced by the particular orthographic features of each language.

Although the recent literature on this issue (Henderson, 1984; Taylor & Taylor, 1983; Tzeng & Hung, 1981) supports this assumption, it should be modified. The acquisition of reading is influenced by language specific differences to a much greater extent than are fluent reading skills. Thus, age and reading ability become important factors in experiments of the sort reported here. Koda does not attempt to control for age or reading ability, or at least has not reported these controls. While not necessarily invalidating her research, age and ability variation may be confounding influences in her study.

Assumption 3: Languages can be classified as requiring phonological recoding, or as allowing direct lexical access from visual recognition to meaning.

There are a number of problems with assuming such a definite classification which are not addressed explicitly in Koda. First, there is only one study of which I am aware (Turvey, Feldman, & Lukatela, 1984) that makes such strong claims for requiring phonological recoding as the only access to the lexicon. The studies on Japanese Kanji/Kana may be problematic because of the mixed uses which they normally serve in Japanese text. Without further evidence for such an extreme view, Turvey et al.'s position must be viewed with some skepticism. Most discussions of phonological mediation in lexical access conclude that phonological mediation might occur but it is not necessary in normal rapid reading (e.g., Banks, Oka, & Shugarman, 1981; Harris & Sipay, 1985; Singer, 1984; Valtin, 1984). The complexity of this assumption is further confounded by two other issues. One was alluded to earlier; that is, the study of reading acquisition is different from the study of mature reading. Many researchers have argued that while phonological mediation occurs in earlier stages of reading development, even in logographic languages (Singer, 1984), fluent readers are less likely to employ phonological mediation for lexical access. Koda, however, does not distinguish among experimental populations in her review discussion of phonological mediation for lexical access. For example, she cites Liberman, Shankweiler, Liberman, Fowler, and Fischer (1977), and Rozin, Poritsky, and Sotsky (1971) to indicate distinctions between Japanese and English phonological mediation strategies. But it must be recognized that subjects in these experiments are children at early stages of reading acquisition. In contrast, Koda uses adults for her study.

The second complexity passed over by Koda is the distinction between the use of phonetic coding for lexical access and for language comprehension. As Valtin notes:

> Phonetic recoding has different relevance for word decoding (identifying the semantic referents of words or word groups belonging together) and for language comprehension (analysing the semantic/syntactic properties of language and combining concepts into meaningful units). While phonetic recoding may be bypassed in word recognition, some sort of speech code is indispensible for the processing of information in working, or short-term memory (1984, p. 228).

Because Koda does not address this issue explicitly, it is not clear whether or not she is collapsing two distinct issues into one. Her discussion of short-term memory research suggests that she is. What differences these issues will have on her study is an open question.

> Assumption 4: The occurrence of a null hypothesis represents a positive argument for a particular position.

The use of the null hypothesis as positive evidence occurs too often in the ESL literature. This happens when a significant finding for a hypothesis is not found, and the author reasons that an alternative hypothesis must therefore hold true. In fact, the null hypothesis finding most often argues for no particular position at all, merely reducing the potential number of explanations by one. To this extent it provides very limited support for any other specific hypothesis. To Koda's credit, she notes the weakness of this approach and concludes that the findings are more suggestive than outrightly supportive of her hypothesis.

Apart from the general review of assumptions underlying Koda's research, there are a few specific issues which I find problematic. In Koda's review of Scribner and Cole (1981), she suggests that different writing systems create individual cognitive differences. Scribner and Cole, in fact, back away from such a major claim (c.f., Singler, 1983). A second problem concerns the description of the subjects in her study. Her student subjects seem to be from fairly diverse English language backgrounds. A discussion of how this group was controlled for English ability levels, exposure to English, age, reading ability in Japanese, and so forth would have been useful.

On the positive side there are two aspects of this study which I find particularly intriguing. First, if students are not affected by phonological interference, then reading time with the two passages in Koda's study should take the same time. Her subjects, however, read the unpronounceable forms significantly faster. I do not know why this increase in speed is the case; it warrants further exploration. Second, the postexperimental debriefing provides some of the more convincing evidence for her study. While self-assessment is notoriously unreliable, the format of the debriefing and the results make such debriefing procedures worth investigating.

From my perspective there do seem to be some problems with the study and the assumptions underlying it. However, this critique also attests to the clarity of the research design and the sophistication of the study. Only a study with a singular, direct purpose, on a major topic in reading research allows exploration of these issues in this depth. More research efforts of this type are needed in ESL reading research. By exploring difficult issues and proposing explicit experimental studies, Koda promotes debate in a useful way. It is debate which will lead us to a more sophisticated account of second language reading acquisition.

References

Banks, Oka, E., & Shugarman, S. (1981). Recoding of printed words to internal speech: Does recoding come before lexical access? In O. Tzeng, & H. Singer (Eds.), *Perception of print* (pp. 137-170). Hillsdale, NJ: Lawrence Erlbaum Associates.

Chaudron, C. (1984, April). What do we mean by 'intake'? On models and methods for discovering learners' processing of input. Paper presented at the 18th Annual TESOL Convention, Houston, TX.

Harris, A., & Sipay, E. (1985). *How to improve reading ability* (8th ed.). New York: Longman.

Henderson, L. (Ed.). (1984). *Orthographies and reading: Perspectives from cognitive psychology, neuropsychology, and linguistics*. Hillsdale, NJ: Lawrence Erlbaum Associates.

Hudelson, S. (Ed.). (1981). *Learning to read in different languages: Series 1, Linguistics and literacy*. Arlington, VA: Center for Applied Linguistics.

Johnston, J., & Hale, B. (1984). The influence of prior context on word identification: Bias and sensitivity effects. In H. Bouma and D. Bouwhis (Eds.), *Attention and Performance X: Control of language processes* (pp. 243-255). Hillsdale, NJ: Lawrence Erlbaum Associates.

Liberman, I. Y., Shankweiler, D., Lieberman, A. M., Fowler, C., & Fishcer, F. W. (1977). Phonetic segmentation and recoding in the beginning reader. In A. S. Reber & D. L. Scarborough (Eds.), *Towards a psychology of reading* (pp. 207-225). Hillsdale, NJ: Lawrence Erlbaum Associates.

McClelland, J., & Rumelhart, D. (1981). An interactive-activation model of the effect of context in perception. Part I: An account of basic findings. *Psychological review, 88*, 375-407.

McLaughlin, B., Rossman, T., & McLeod, B. (1983). Second language learning: An information-processing perspective. *Language learning, 33*, 135-158.

Monsell, S. (1984). Components of working memory underlying verbal skills: A 'distributed capacities' view—A tutorial review." In H. Bouma & D. Bouwhuis (Eds.), *Attention and performance X: Control of language processes* (pp. 327-350). Hillsdale, NJ: Lawrence Erlbaum Associates.

Pearson, P. D. (Ed.). (1984). *Handbook of reading research*. New York: Longman.

Rozin, P., Poritsky, S., & Sotsky, R. (1971). American children with reading problems can easily learn to read English represented by Chinese characters. *Science, 171*, 1264-1267.

Scribner, S., & Cole, M. (1981). *The psychology of literacy*. Cambridge, MA: Harvard University.

Singer, H. (1984). Learning to read and skilled reading: Multiple system interacting within and between the reader and the text. In J. Downing & R. Valtin (Eds.), *Language awareness and learning to read* (pp. 193-206). New York: Springer-Verlag.

Singler, J. (1983). Review of The psychology of literacy. *Language, 59*, 893-901.

Taylor, I., & Taylor, B. (1983). *The psychology of reading*. New York: Academic Press.

Turvey, M., Feldman, L., & Lukatela, G. (1984). The Serbo-Croatian orthography constrains the reader to a phonologically analytic strategy. In L. Henderson (Ed.), *Orthographies and reading: Perspectives from cognitive psychology, neuropsychology, and linguistics* (pp. 81-89). Hillsdale, NJ: Lawrence Erlbaum Associates.

Tzeng, O., & Hung, D. (1981). Linguistic determinism: A written language perspective. In O. Tzeng & H. Singer (Eds.), *Perception of print* (pp. 237-255). Hillsdale, NJ: Lawrence Erlbaum Associates.

Valtin, R. (1984). Awareness of features and functions of language. In J. Dowing & R. Valtin (Eds.), *Language awareness and learning to read* (pp. 227-260). New York: Springer-Verlag.

The Relationship Between Nonverbal Schematic Concept Formation and Story Comprehension

Kyle Perkins

Southern Illinois University

The Relationship Between Nonverbal Schematic Concept Formation and Story Comprehension

This investigation focuses on the relationship between English as a Second Language (ESL) readers' performance on a schematic concept formation task (SCF) and their performance on a reading task. The aspect of the reading task investigated in this study is the reader's knowledge of a text's conventional structure.

Perceptual learning theorists working in the area of psychophysics have studied the pattern recognition approach to schema learning which has its origin in the work of Bartlett (1932), Woodworth (1938), Attneave (1957), and Evans (1967a). Bartlett is credited with introducing the basic idea of the schema. Woodworth extended Bartlett's idea by claiming that persons categorize new stimuli and objects into general classes (schemata) and then note the correction or exception of the stimulus in relation to the schema. Attneave contributed the notions of the communality of the schema and of deviation from the central tendency as correction or exception of newly perceived stimuli in relation to the schema.

Evans (1967a, b) has carried forward Attneave's view of deviation from the central tendency of previous experience in terms of how a new experience deviates from the previously developed communality by introducing the concept of SCF. Evans' SCF concerns pattern classification as the spontaneous development of a prototype (schema) from an array of stimuli. When subjects form a schematic concept, they extract the relevant patterned stimulation from a corpus of stimuli or events. Evans defines a schema as "a characteristic of some population of objects...a set of rules which would serve as instructions for producing a population prototype and object typical of the population" (1967a, p. 77).

In Evans' framework a schema family is a population of objects which can be described in terms of their deviations from a prototype. The SCF paradigm involves the assignment of objects to their corresponding schema families. A subject must first conceptualize the schema family to which the objects belong and then assign the objects to their corresponding schema families on the basis of information derived from the perception of the objects. No prior familiarization with the relevant schemata is presumed. In an SCF paradigm, an array of stimulus patterns is presented to a subject who must abstract a schema or schemata and then assign the stimulus objects to one classification or another.

In terms of application, SCF tasks have been employed as measures of general learning ability (Price & Evans, 1972), and good readers have been shown to perform better on SCF tasks than poor readers (Lane, Evans, & Lane, 1974).

There is a rich tradition of textual analysis research which focuses on a reader's knowledge of the conventional structure of different types of text known as *story schema*. Numerous researchers have reported on the roles that a story schema plays such as organizing the incoming information during the reading comprehension process and directing inferential and temporal processing during the retrieval process (e.g., Rumelhart, 1975; Stein & Glenn, 1979).

The previously cited research by Evans (1967a, b), Lane, Evans, and Lane (1974), Rumelhart (1975), and Stein and Glenn (1979) provided the impetus for the research reported in this paper. The present study was designed to explore the relationship between SCF and reading performance with an ESL subject pool and to answer the following research questions: (a) Would there be a stable and predictable relationship between schema formation and reading comprehension performance? (b) Would there be a significant difference between high ability SCF subjects' and low ability SCF subjects' scores on the reading measure? and (c) Would there be a significant difference in the subjects' responses to questions based on different category types of information found in the story grammars of the texts used in the reading measure?

Method

Subjects

Subjects were 22 advanced-level adult ESL students enrolled in full-time intensive English classes at the Center for English as a Second Language at Southern Illinois University with the following distribution of native languages: Arabic, 4; Chinese, 3; Japanese, 2; Korean, 4; Malay, 1; Spanish, 6; Somali, 1; Thai, 1. Students in the advanced-level proficiency stratum can read the same general, nontechnical materials as a native-speaking college freshman. The reading materials for this level of student are about the length of a short story and incorporate a broader vocabulary as well as contextual clues. Students at this level can cope with concrete as well as abstract ideas and are able to distinguish their own ideas from those of the author. The subjects' average TOEFL score was 487.18; their average TOEFL reading comprehension and vocabulary score was 46.85.

Materials

Selby H. Evans of Texas Christian University generated the graphic stimuli for this research. The stimuli were sampled from a defined population composed of variants which are independent and measurable deviations from a well-defined prototype or schema. There were four prototypes (four schema families) and a set of nine instances was generated at a 70% redundancy to illustrate each of the four prototypes, resulting in a total of 36 stimuli; see Appendix A. The four SCF prototypes are presented in Figure 1.

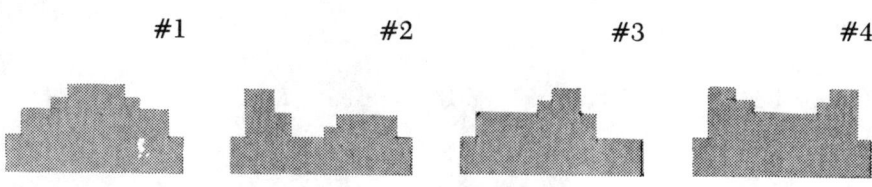

Figure 1: SCF—The Four Prototypes

Five stories were used in the study. The five stories, on average 225 words long, and the comprehension questions for each story came from an ESL test battery developed by Grant H. Henning (1981).[1]

All of the statements in each of the five stories were parsed into the categories specified by the story grammar presented in Stein and Glenn (1979). The internal structure of a story consists of a setting and one or more episodes. An episode contains an initiating event, a response, a plan sequence, a resolution, a consequence, and a reaction.

Two independent, anonymous raters parsed each story, and the interrater reliability of the two raters' parsing was estimated at 0.85. Tree structures derived from the Stein and Glenn (1979) analysis were drawn for each of the five stories, and each of the 30 reading comprehension questions was matched to the statement and its category type on which it was based. The text of Story 1, its tree structure, and its comprehension questions are presented as Appendices B, C, and D.

Procedure

Working time was 5 minutes for the SCF and 50 minutes for the reading comprehension test. Both were administered during a single class period. The subject pool came from two different classes, and the two measures were presented in a counterbalanced order.

Results

Table 1. Means, Standard Deviations, and Estimates of Reliability

Measure	Mean	Standard Deviation	Type of Reliability	Estimate of Reliability
Schematic Concept Formation	77.71	14.28	KR-20	0.8176
Reading Comprehension	73.59	15.15	KR-20	0.8183

$r = 0.8066$

The means, standard deviations, and Kuder-Richardson 20 internal consistency estimates of reliability for the item responses from the two measures are presented in Table 1.

To determine whether there was a stable and predictable relationship between schema formation and reading comprehension performance, the proportion of the reliable variance which is shared by the two measures was computed. An r^2 "corrected for unreliability" of 0.97 was obtained.

The SCF item responses were submitted to Rasch one-parameter latent trait measurement to estimate person ability measures corrected for test width expansion for all subjects (Wright & Stone, 1979). The Rasch analysis indicated that there were 14 high-ability persons and 8 low-ability persons on the SCF measure.

The reading responses were submitted to a two-way analysis of variance with one entry per cell with a repeated measurements design. The analysis was conducted to determine: (a) whether there was a significant difference between the high-ability SCF subjects' and the low-ability SCF subjects' scores on the reading measure and (b) whether there was a significant difference in the subjects' responses to questions based on different category types of information found in the story grammar of the texts.

The data for the ANOVA and the summary table for the ANOVA are presented in Tables 2 and 3. There was a significant effect due to SCF ability levels, $F(1,7) = 45.54$, $p < .05$, but there was no significant effect due to the different category types, $F(7,7) = 2.56$, n.s.

Table 2. Data for ANOVA

	Category Types (Factor B)							Effect of Ability Levels
	Major Setting	Minor Setting	Initiating Event	Internal Response	Attempt	Internal Plan	Direct Conseq.	Reaction	
High Ability SCF Subjects	75	78	74	93	79	86	77	86	$\bar{X} = 81$
SCF Ability Levels (Factor A)									
Low Ability SCF Subjects	64	54	56	75	71	62	47	53	$\bar{X} = 60$
Effect of Category Types	$\bar{X} = 71$	70	68	86	76	77	66	74	

$\bar{X}$ Grand = 74

Table 3. Summary Table for ANOVA for Responses Related to Ability Levels and Category Types

Source of variation	df	Sum of Squares	Mean Squares	F
Ability levels	1	1722.25	1722.25	45.54*
Category Types	7	678.75	96.96	2.56
Interaction	7	264.75	37.82	
Total	15	2665.75	XXX	

*$p<.05$

Separate ANOVA were computed for each of the five stories to determine if there were a significant effect for category types. The analyses shown in Table 4 indicated a significant effect for category types in stories 2 and 5.

Discussion

The results of this investigation suggest that an ESL student who exhibits proficiency in a nonverbal task of finding the common features which constitute a single pattern or multiple patterns in a set of stimuli which represent two or more classes and of assigning those stimuli to their prototypes also possesses attained proficiency in the conventional structure of simple stories. This internalized story structure competence can be attributed to experience and/or overt classroom instruction. It is presumed that the structure of simple stories can be arrayed as a hierarchical network of categories serving differential functions in a story structure and of the logical relations existing between and within these categories.

There is a parallel between nonverbal SCF and story comprehension, as can be inferred from the following account of discourse processing:

> The process of understanding discourse is the process of finding a configuration of schemata that offers an adequate account of the passage in question . . . Clues from the story suggest possible interpretations (instantiations of schemata) that are then evaluated against the successive sentences of the story until finally a consistent interpretation is discovered (Rumelhart, 1980, p. 47).

The results of determining the proportion of reliable shared variance between the SCF and the reading measure suggest that a subject who performs a nonverbal SCF task and who controls the conventional structure of simple

Table 4. ANOVA for Category Types for Each Story

Story 1 $F(3,63) = -10.48$	Initiating Event (3 items)	Attempt (1 item)	Major Setting (1 item)	Internal Response (1 item)
2 $F(3,63) = 8.41*$	Attempt (1 item)	Reaction (1 item)	Direct Consequence (2 items)	Minor Setting (2 items)
3 $F(2,42) = 2.74$	Major Setting (4 items)	Direct Consequence (1 item)	Minor Setting (1 item)	
4 $F(3,63) = 0.16$	Initiating Event (3 items)	Internal Plan (1 item)	Minor Setting (1 item)	Attempt (1 item)
5 $F(3,63) = 7.48*$	Major Setting (1 item)	Direct Consequence (1 item)	Reaction (3 items)	Initiating Event (1 item)

* $p < .05$

stories makes use of the same operations: forming hypotheses about the schema families (prototypes) and finding the common features, that is evaluating the goodness to fit of hypotheses (schemata) that account for the different characteristics of the text or evaluating the goodness to fit of different stimuli to schema families in the case of the nonverbal graphic stimuli.

Further analyses reported indicated that there was a significant difference in the subjects' responses to questions based on different category types of information found in the grammars for stories 2 and 5. Separate Chi-square tests were run for the observations from each of the two stories. The expected frequencies were determined for each category type, and those frequencies were compared with the observed frequencies.

For Story 2, the obtained X^2 with the Yates correction factor for the high ability SCF subjects' responses to a question based on a minor setting statement was $X^2 = 4.45$, 1 df, $p < .05$. A similar Chi-square test for the low ability SCF subjects' responses was not significant, that is there was no difference between their expected and observed frequencies of responses.

The question based on a minor setting statement in Story 2 dealt with the main character's being on duty. The difficulty index for this item was 0.23. In order to infer that Trent was a policeman on duty and on patrol, the subjects needed a "policeman on patrol" schema. The story contained clues necessary to interpret the appropriate schema such as "Sergeant Trent" and "reached for his pocket radio and called the police station." It appears that the subject pool experienced difficulty with this particular question because they did not have the appropriate schema (Rumelhart, 1980).

The troublesome category type in Story 5 was a major setting which had a difficulty index of 0.27. A Chi-square test indicated no significant difference between expected and observed frequencies for either ability level. Whether the subjects had the appropriate schema and sufficient clues for interpretation is not at issue.

The stem for the major setting question was "On weekdays Maria usually left her bed at _____" (correct response = "before half past seven"). The text indicated that Maria always woke up at 7:15 on weekdays and was ready to get out of bed within a quarter of an hour. It could be argued that this item is an invalid measure of reading because it assesses simple arithmetic.

It has been presumed throughout this paper that those subjects who control the conventional structure (story grammar) of simple stories are more proficient readers than those subjects who do not. In doing empirical research, however, one must always be aware of rival, competing hypotheses which can also explain the data. There are other factors that could explain the differential performance of the subjects in the two ability levels in this study: (a) a lack of automaticity in word identification, (b) rigidity in perception and conceptualization, (c) a lack of mundane information, (d) a lack of variable depth processing, (e) a lack of interaction between textual structural knowledge and general world knowledge, (f) an inability to introduce strategic activity, and (g) an inability to comprehend the questions.

LaBerge and Samuels (1976) note that some readers are able to achieve word identification automatically, while other readers struggle with words as they read. The reading passages employed in this research may have contained many novel vocabulary items for the lower ability subjects, and they might not have developed automaticity at word identification. Since a reader has a limited amount of available processing capacity, the reader who devotes considerable attention to word identification has little time left to devote to meaning comprehension.

Robinson (1964) has investigated rigidity and conceptualization in reading comprehension. She hypothesized that most readers are flexible in their perception and conceptualization; however, it may be the case that the lower-level ability subjects relied principally upon a single perceptual and conceptual style which they could not modify, and the net result was a reduction of comprehension.

There is a great deal of mundane, taken-for-granted knowledge that a reader must bring to the comprehension process for a text to be comprehended. Pearson and Johnson (1978) refer to this information as a script. Scripts include information about conventions, physical causality, societal norms, and human intentionality. The lower-level subjects may have lacked scripts or have had incomplete scripts for the reading passages due to their relatively brief exposure to English. It seems that scripts are built up through long-term experience and exposure to the language.

Dehn (1984) observes that reading is not a uniform process because during proficient comprehension, the reader ignores less important information and processes more deeply the material which really warrants it. The reader who does this is capable of variable depth processing (Schank, 1978). The lower level subjects may not have been able to determine which parts of the stimulus paragraphs merited considerable processing and which did not.

One probable source of difficulty for the lower-level subjects was their inability to control text structural information in the test passages. A critical aspect of reading comprehension is the interaction of structural knowledge and general world knowledge:

> Subjects read texts one line at a time, and after each line, stated how they believed the text would continue from that point. When these anticipation responses were scored against the actual continuation of the text, two trends were evident. First, the likelihood of a correct anticipation increased as the reader progressed through the text, suggesting that the information acquired increasingly constrained the possible ways that the text could develop. Second, the places where correct anticipations were generated were characterized by the presence of considerable world and text-structural knowledge (Kintsch & Miller, 1984, p. 228).

Brown (1980) notes that a proficient reader introduces strategic activity during the reading process in order to improve cognitive economy and to improve the expenditure of effort. According to Brown, the efficient reader must evaluate strategy selection in order to analyze the textual information only to the extent necessary to meet current needs. It may be the case that the lower-level ability readers were less prone to introduce strategic activity.

When subjects answer a reading comprehension question, they must understand the original test passage from which the question was derived, and they must also understand the question itself. According to Lehnert (1978), understanding what a reading comprehension question calls for can be a complex activity. Even after the subject understands what a question asks, s/he uses a reconstructive process to retrieve the answer from short or long term memory (Xolodner, 1980). Understanding the questions may have entailed skills which were not the point of the questions and which were beyond the ken of the lower level ability subjects. A lack of story grammar facility plus any one or a combination of these factors may account for the differential reading performance of the subjects from the two different ability levels reported in this research.

In an earlier section of this paper it was shown that the proportion of reliable variance common to the SCF and the reading comprehension measure was estimated at 0.9726. It is tempting to claim that these two measures are assessing the same construct; however, that claim could be overdrawn and spurious for the following reasons.

Suppose that two constructs, X and Y, are correlated by reason of a causative relation to a common variable, E, but that they are not perfectly correlated because each is also caused, in part, by different variables, L and M, which are themselves uncorrelated:

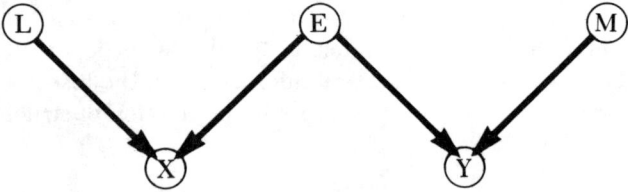

where
- L = general intelligence
- E = general learning ability
- M = overt classroom instruction
- X = SCF
- Y = story comprehension

General intelligence is suggested as a variable because "the best single explanatory principle for observed variance in reading skills [is] variance in general intelligence" (Lohnes and Gray, 1972, p. 59).

Measures of X and Y, x and y, will be correlated if they are at all reliable: $r_{xx}>0$, $r_{yy}>0$, in the following fashion: (error terms are by definition uncorrelated).

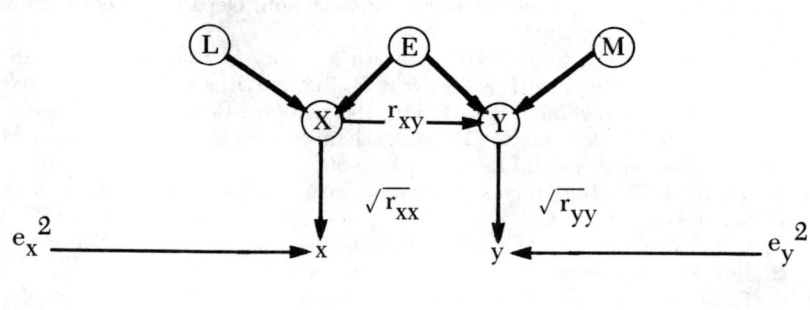

$$r_{xy} = \sqrt{r_{xx}} \cdot \sqrt{r_{yy}} \cdot r_{xy}$$

(where the variables are normalized). This is the common "correction for attentuation."

An interesting area for further research would be to test the appropriateness of this causal model by using path analysis and structural equation models. The object of this investigation would be to determine how much variance in the constructs underlying story comprehension is due to instruction, general learning, ability, general intelligence, SCF, and unmeasured residual sources.

References

Attneave, F. (1957). Transfer of experience with a class-schema to identification learning of patterns and shapes. *Journal of Experimental Psychology, 54*, 81-88.

Bartlett, F. C. (1932). *Remembering: A study in experimental and social psychology.* Cambridge: Cambridge University Press.

Brown, A. L. (1980). Metacognitive development and reading. In R. J. Spiro, N. C. Bruce, W. F. Brewer (Eds.), *Theoretical issues in reading comprehension.* Hillsdale, NJ: Lawrence Erlbaum Associates.

Dehn, N. (1984). An AI perspective on reading comprehension. In J. Flood (Ed.), *Understanding reading comprehension: Cognition, language, and the structure of prose.* Newark, DE: International Reading Association.

Evans, S. H. (1967a). A brief statement of schema theory. *Psychonomic Science, 8*, 87-88.

Evans, S. H. (1967b). Redundancy as a variable in pattern recognition. *Psychological Bulletin, 67*, 104-113.

Henning, G. (1981). *AUC EFL proficiency test.* Unpublished Manuscript, American University in Cairo, English Language Institute, Cairo.

Kintsch, W., & Miller, J. R. (1984). Readability: A view from cognitive psychology. In J. Flood (Ed.), *Understanding reading comprehension: Cognition, language and the structure of prose*. Newark, DE: International Reading Association.

Kolodner, J. (1980). *Retrieval and organizational strategies in conceptual memory: A computer model*. Unpublished doctoral dissertation, Department of Computer Science, Yale University.

Laberge, D., & Samuels, S. J. (1976). Toward a theory of automatic information processing in reading. In H. Singer & R. B. Ruddell (Eds.), *Theoretical models and processes of reading*, Newark, DE: International Reading Association.

Lane, S., Evans, S. H., & Lane, C. (1974). A schema theory approach to the reading process. *The Psychological Record, 24,* 75-80.

Lehnert, W. G. (1978). *The process of question answering*. Hillsdale, NJ: Lawrence Erlbaum Associates.

Lohnes, P. R., & Gray, M. M. (1972). Intelligence and the cooperative reading studies. *Reading Research Quarterly, 7,* 466-476.

Pearson, P. D., & Johnson, D. D. (1978). *Teaching reading comprehension*. New York: Holt, Reinhart, and Winston.

Price, J., & Evans, S. H. (1972, September). Schematic concept formation as a predictor of success in a remedial education program. *Technical Memorandum,* 22-72.

Robinson, H. M. (1964). Perceptual and conceptual style related to reading. In J. A. Figuerel (Ed.), *Improvement of reading through classroom instruction* (pp. 26-28). Newark, DE: International Reading Association.

Rumelhart, D. E. (1975). Notes on a schema for stories. In D. G. Brown & A. Collins (Eds.), *Representation and understanding: Studies in cognitive science*. New York: Academic Press.

Rumelhart, D. E. (1980). Schemata: The building blocks of cognition. In R. Spiro, B. C. Bruce, & W. F. Brewer (Eds.), *Theoretical issues in reading comprehension: Perspectives and cognitive psychology, linguistics, artificial intelligence, and education*. Hillsdale, NJ: Lawrence Erlbaum Associates.

Schank, R. (1978). *Interestingness: Controlling inferences*. (Research report #145). New Haven, CT: Yale University, Department of Computer Sciences.

Stein, N. L., & Glenn, C. G. (1979). An analysis of story comprehension in elementary school children. In R. O. Freedle (Ed.), *New directions in discourse processing, Vol. 2*. Norwood, NJ: Ablex.

Woodworth, R. (1938). *Experimental psychology*. New York: Holt.

Wright, B. D., & Stone, M. H. (1979). *Best test design: Rasch measurement*. Chicago: Mesa.

Footnote

[1]The first story concerned a haughty, young, rich girl who was embarrassed by the appearance of her ugly mother at a graduation ceremony at a rich Swiss boarding school for girls. The second story related the episode of a policeman, Trent, on patrol who managed to thwart what he thought was a robbery in progress. The "robbery" turned out to be a movie scene. The third story was about a young boy on his way to visit relatives in a distant city. Upon his arrival at his destination, he saw no one was there to meet him, and he became terribly upset. The fourth story was an adventure in the sky about a passenger who landed a plane after the pilot had taken ill. The fifth story was about a female nonnative student who was concerned that her English was not good enough to explain a nonthreatening illness to an English-speaking doctor.

Appendix A
SCF Stimuli Array

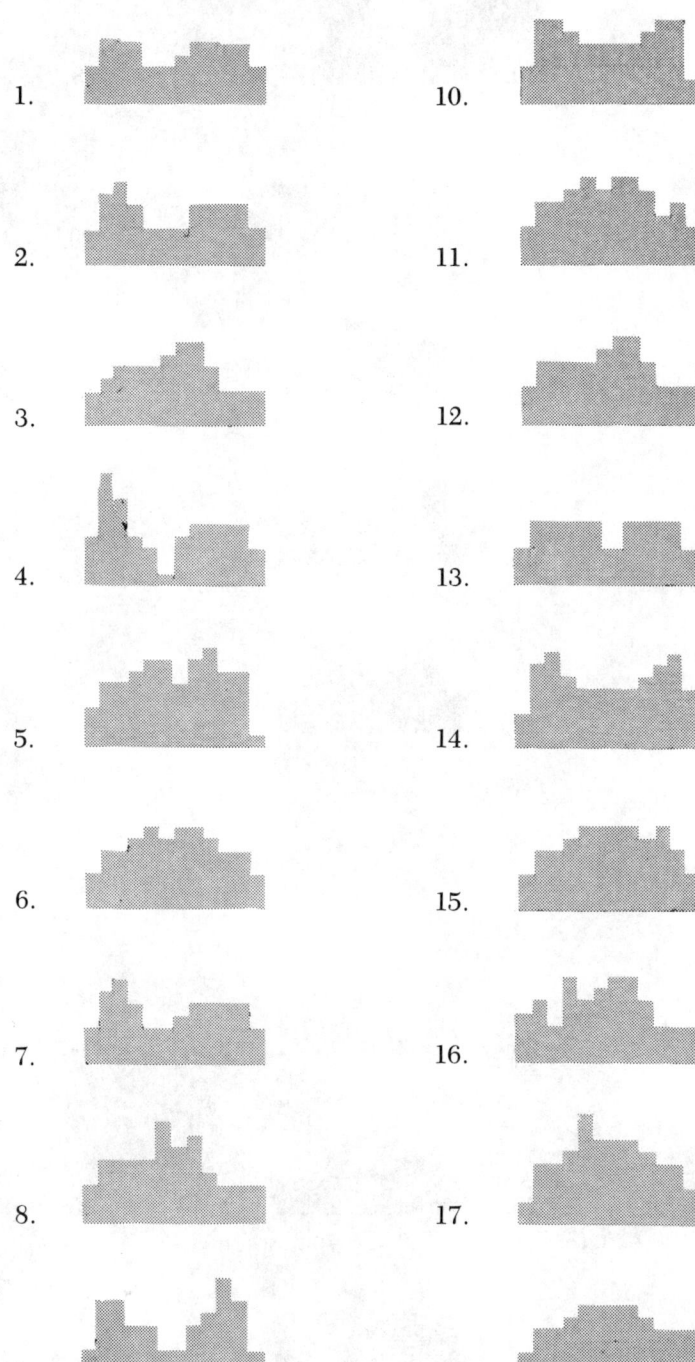

166 NONVERBAL SCHEMATIC CONCEPT FORMATION
Appendix A
SCF Stimuli Array

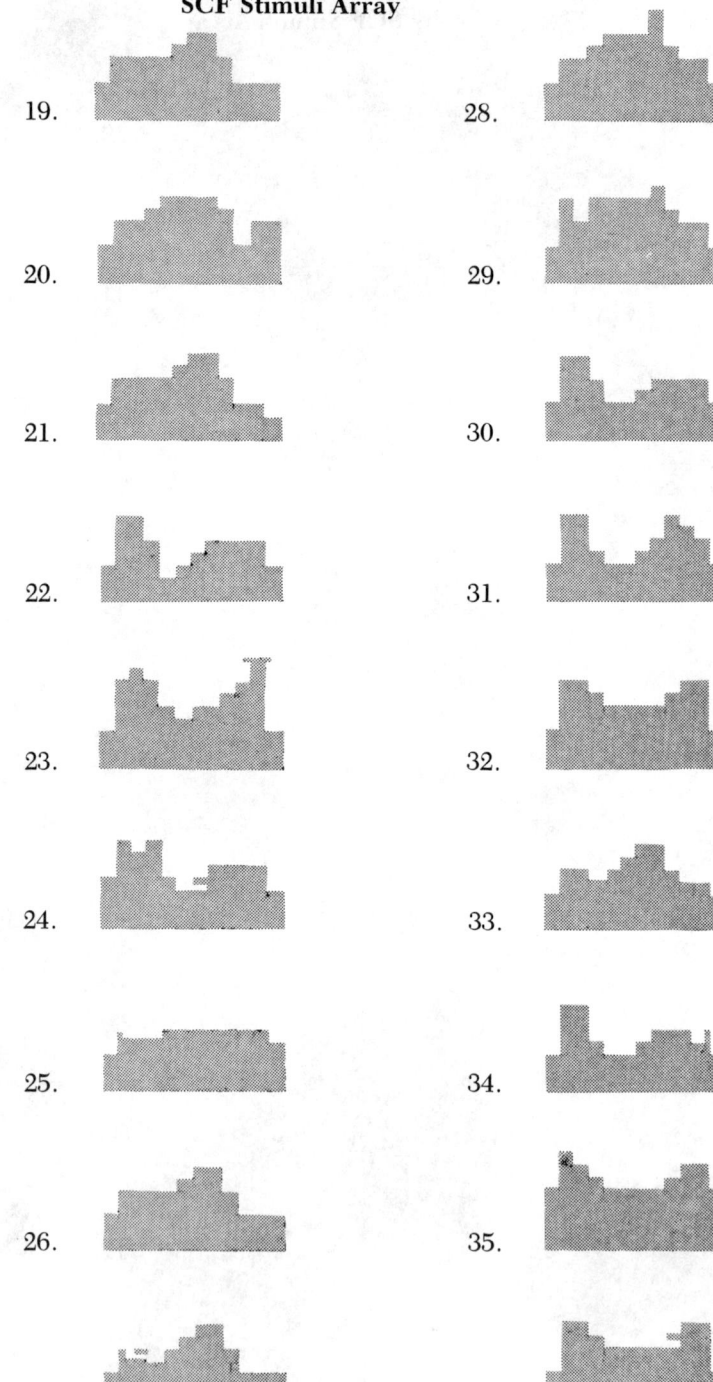

Appendix B
Text of Story 1: <u>Nancy</u>

Category Type	Type of Information	Statement
Major Setting	State	1. Nancy was a foreign student in an expensive Swiss school for girls.
Major Setting	State	2. In her class of sixteen-year-olds, she was the prettiest and fairest.
Minor Setting	State	3. Most of the girls were rich
Minor Setting	Action	4. and went to school in cars driven by chauffeurs.
Minor Setting	State	5. When it was graduation day
Minor Setting	Action	6. all parents came to school
Minor Setting	Action	7. to watch their children
Minor Setting	Action	8. receive their diplomas.
Major Setting	Action	9. In the middle of the ceremony an old woman with marks of an old wound on her face walked into the hall.
Major Setting	Action	10. Everyone looked at her
Internal Plan	Subgoal	11. as she went
Attempt	Action	12. to take a seat by Nancy
Major Setting	State	13. who was sitting in the front row.
Direct Consequence	Action	14. Very quickly, the girl showed her a seat in the last row.
Major Setting	Action	15. At the end of the ceremony the ugly woman overheard Nancy
Initiating Event	Action	16. explaining to her friends that she was an old servant of her family.
Direct Consequence	Action	17. With tears running down her cheek
Direct Consequence	Action	18. the old woman ran out of the hall.
Initiating Event	Internal Event	19. Nancy knew then that her mother ( ) had overheard the conversation.
Major Setting	State	20. (whom she had not seen for six years)
Internal Plan	Subgoal	21. She hurried behind her.
Internal Plan	Subgoal	22. When she caught up with her mother,
Attempt	Action	23. she apologized for her unkind words.

168 NONVERBAL SCHEMATIC CONCEPT FORMATION

Appendix C
Tree Structure for Story 1: <u>Nancy</u>

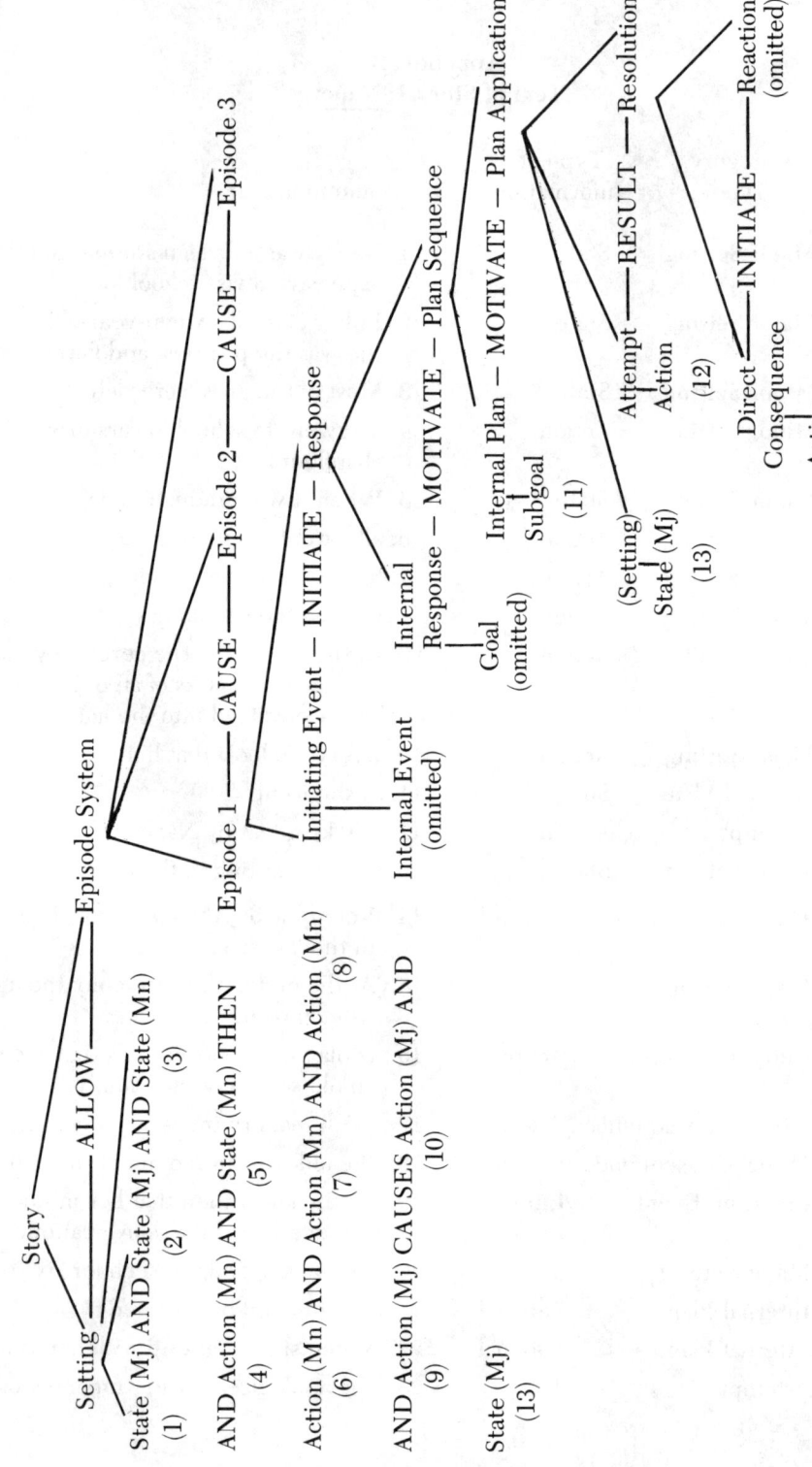

Appendix C
(cont.)

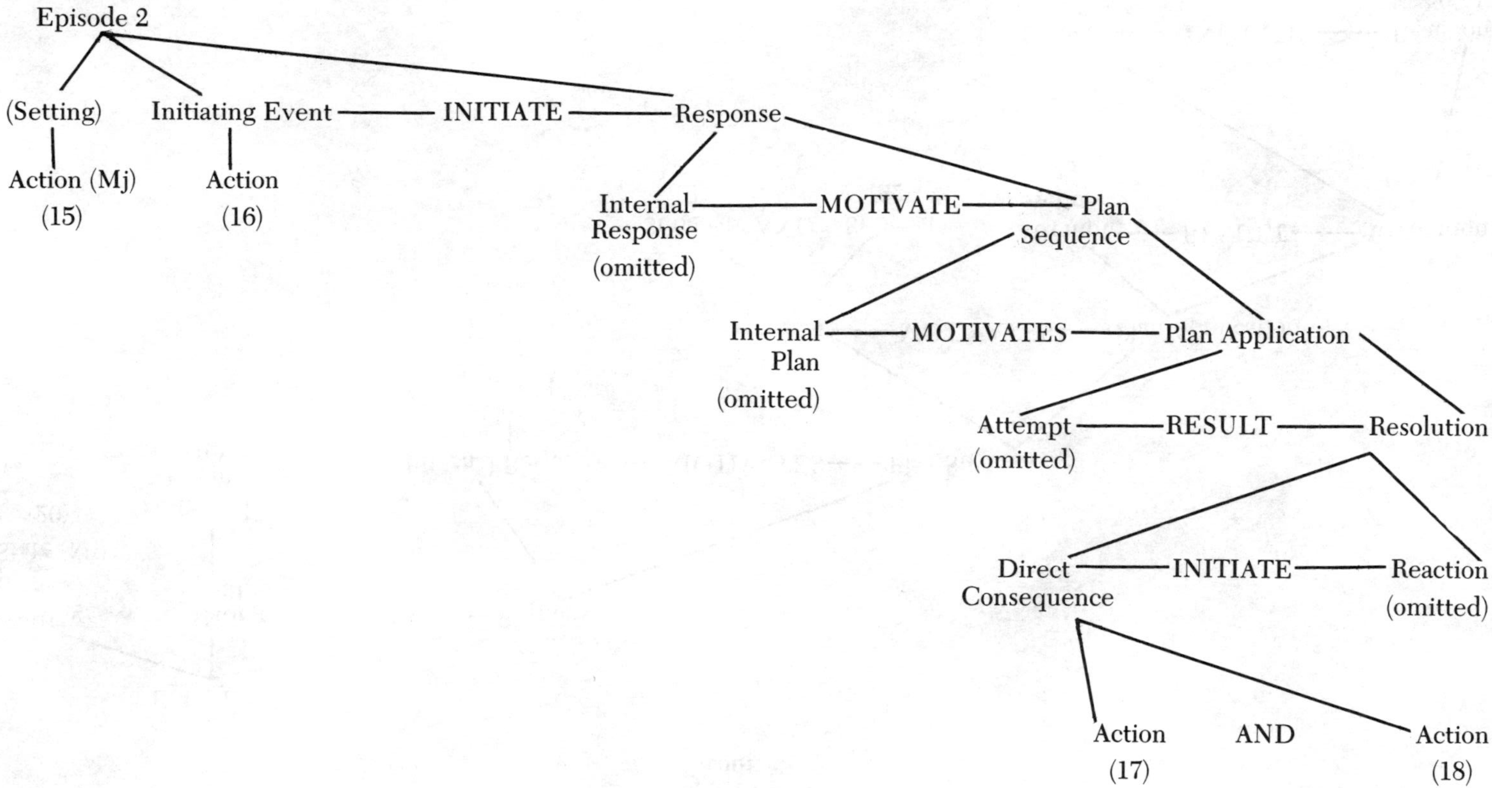

Episode 2
├── (Setting) — Action (Mj) (15)
└── Initiating Event — Action (16)
    └── INITIATE — Response
        ├── Internal Response (omitted)
        └── MOTIVATE — Plan Sequence
            ├── Internal Plan (omitted)
            └── MOTIVATES — Plan Application
                ├── Attempt (omitted)
                └── RESULT — Resolution
                    ├── Reaction (omitted)
                    └── INITIATE — Direct Consequence
                        └── AND
                            ├── Action (17)
                            └── Action (18)

Appendix C
(cont.)

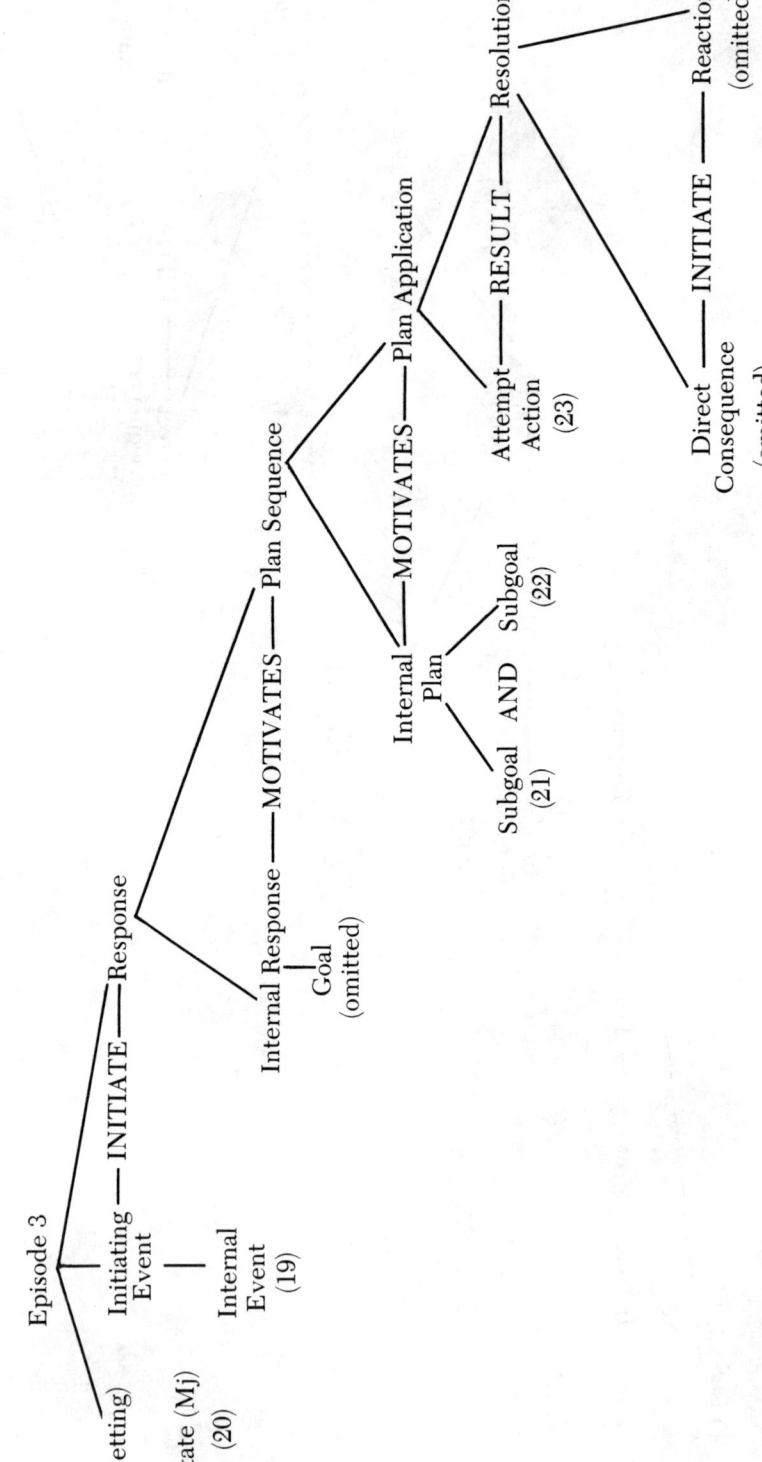

Appendix D
Questions for Story 1

1. Who was the old woman?
   a) Nancy's old servant
   b) Nancy's mother
   c) Nancy's friend
   d) Nancy's school mistress

2. Nancy asked the woman to sit in the back because _____ .
   a) she was ashamed of her.
   b) she wanted to be with her friends.
   c) the woman came late.
   d) all the parents sat in the back.

3. Nancy apologized to the lady because _____ .
   a) the lady was old.
   b) she had been away for six years.
   c) she hurt her feelings.
   d) there wasn't a seat in the front row.

4. All the girls in the class were _____ .
   a) Swiss
   b) pretty
   c) poor
   d) young

5. The old lady ran out of the hall because _____ .
   a) she was disappointed with Nancy.
   b) her seat was uncomfortable.
   c) she wasn't a mother.
   d) of her hurry to see her chauffeur.

6. When the old woman left the hall, Nancy _____ .
   a) realized she had made a mistake.
   b) saw the old wound on her face.
   c) told her classmates who she was.
   d) had tears in her eyes.

Comments on Perkins

Andrew D. Cohen

Hebrew University of Jerusalem

This paper reminds us that cognitive processes in reading are linked to general cognitive processes, that is, classifying stimuli into general classes (referred to in this paper as schema or prototypes, terms which Bartlett did not use in 1932). The study demonstrated that the link between a nonverbal classifying task and a language (reading) classifying task was quite high. It is impressive to see that the link was so strong, especially when research elsewhere (Naiman, Forlilch, Stern, & Toderco, 1978) has not yielded high correlations between nonverbal tests of cognitive processing (e.g., the hidden figures test) and language processing tasks.

But then we may ask, "If the fit is so high, so what?" In other words, what do we do with this finding? Are we to give the schematic concept formation task to students to predict how well they will understand stories? It would appear that this measure could be used to predict their ability to do a number of other tasks as well.

Actually, this study did not show the schematic concept formation (SCF) task to tease out category differences within the story grammar task. This reinforces the notion that high/low SCF ability is not finely tuned to language processing. Also, we are dealing here with only one genre of text, that is text conventional structure for stories. College students need to read more than stories. In fact, in many areas of specialization, story structure would be irrelevant.

Perkins is most helpful in reminding us that successful performance on a schema task in reading (30 reading comprehension questions supposedly depending on schema knowledge for successful response) may actually also depend on a number of other factors: vocabulary knowledge; perceptual/conceptual style, which includes schema; scripts/world knowledge; extensiveness of processing different parts of the text; use of strategies; and the quality of the reading questions, not just of the passage. These were not explored in this study.

Even though the correlation between the SCF task results and the reading task results was extremely high, it would appear that other types of studies would be beneficial in order to better understand the nature of the findings. One such approach would be to obtain verbal reports from the readers to see where they think their problems lie. It would also be beneficial to introduce story retelling in place of reading comprehension questions, since the latter could have distorted the results.

References

Bartlett, F. C. (1932). *Remembering: A study in experimental and social psychology.* Cambridge: Cambridge University Press.

Naiman, N., Forlilch, M., Stern, H. H., & Toderco, A. (1978). *The good language learner.* Toronto: Modern Language Center, Ontario Institute for Studies in Education.

ESL Reading Pedagogy:
Implications of Schema-Theoretical Research

Mark O. James

Brigham Young University - Hawaii Campus

ESL Reading Pedagogy: Implications of Schema-Theoretical Research

Over the past 15 years we have learned a great deal about the reading process. Researchers generally agree that during the previous 200 years there was too much concern with the text. Scholars were a long time in discovering that though reading had much to do with the printed page, reading comprehension did not. The important difference in these terms will soon become apparent.

Today, most people will agree that reading has much more to do with the reader than it does with readability formulas. What was once thought to be a one-way flow of information to the brain is now known to be an interactive, or two-way, communication between the reader's mind and the information printed. The subsequent emphasis on the product rather than the process of reading has led to the development of materials and practices that merely test reading comprehension, but do not teach it.

Scholars have come to acknowledge that the text in and of itself is meaningless. In other words, it is the reader who assigns meaning. A text can have as many shades of meaning as there are readers—each interprets the information according to his or her perceptions and experiences, prior knowledge, and past reading. This newly-recognized idiosyncratic nature of reading has made it an even more elusive process than it seemed 20 years ago. Yet, we have made great strides recently in understanding how readers contribute to the reading process.

Although there are several new and exciting paths of research today, I will discuss only one, schema-theoretical research, and the contributions it has made and can make to classroom pedagogy. Schema-theoretical research is the study of the influence of schema or prior knowledge structures on comprehension and recall (for a full review, see Carrell, 1983a). The concept of schema can be simply demonstrated. Glance briefly at the following sequence of letters:

T G C I M E P W S Q

Now without looking back, write down as many of the letters in their proper sequence as you can.

Now glance briefly at this next sequence of letters:

A B C D E F G H I J

Now without looking back, write down as many of the letters in their proper sequence as you can.

Because the second sequence matches up with at least a part of a knowledge structure already acquired by most speakers of English, we can readily assimilate the second series of data. To one who is not familiar with the English alphabet, on the other hand, there is no inherent advantage to the second series.

A second major property of schema is demonstrated by a drawing which can be interpreted, depending on first impression or prior instruction, as either a young fashionable lady or an old witch. Try as you might it is most difficult to convince someone that you see something different. Our prior ideas can restrict our perceptions and even create a resistance to new ideas or viewpoints that are inconsistent with the original. The implications that these two properties have for the process of reading will be discussed below. But first let us review the nature of recent research in the area of schema.

According to the schema theory, the process of comprehension is guided by the idea that input is overlaid upon preexisting knowledge in an attempt to find a match. There are two simultaneous processes occurring here. One is called bottom-up processing and involves the movement of data from the page to the brain. This upward movement triggers certain past experiences or perceptions about the topic.

The other process is called top-down processing and represents an attempt by the brain to find an existing knowledge structure to superimpose onto the incoming data in order to more quickly facilitate the assimilation of this new information. These two processes share a symbiotic or complementary relationship; that is, the one is not able to function properly without the other. The top-down processing works, however, only when the reader's schema matches the incoming data. If the data contradicts the reader's schema, one of two things can happen. Either the schema is amended by the new information, or the information is rejected in favor of the existing schema.

There are basically three areas of schema that play a part in the act of reading. There are linguistic schema, content schema, and formal schema. *Linguistic schema* is the knowledge of the letters and their corresponding sounds, both alone and in clusters; a reader's familarity with the frequency of various letter clusters; and the ability to predict, through the knowledge of syntax, the word or words that will follow. A great percentage of what we refer to as reading instruction—phonics, grammar, word attack skills, letter recognition, vocabulary, and cloze exercises—is geared toward this area of knowledge.

The second type of knowledge structure—*content schema*—refers to a reader's knowledge about the topic being read or discussed. Studies show that readers comprehend more of a text if: (a) They are already familiar with the topic from experience; (b) they have read something about the topic before; and (c) they know in advance what reading concerns.

I think all of us have read something that we were not familiar with, and found it quite difficult. I had this experience just a while ago while reading a "how to" book on electrical wiring. No matter how many times I read it, or how slowly I read it, I could not comprehend it to any functional degree.

Thelen (1982) makes a useful distinction between reading problems and comprehension problems. It was neither my lack of knowledge concerning the grammar of the English language, nor of the vocabulary (I knew the meaning of the words, give or take one or two); yet, I could not make sense of it. Thelen would argue that I did not have a reading problem per se; it was a comprehension problem. Linguistic schema are associated with the former, content and formal schema with the latter.

Where does the solution lie? In the text? In the reader? Schema theory would say most likely the latter. It would not help for me to study vocabulary nor grammar. Nor would it help for someone to adapt the story in order to fit some readability scale. I do not understand the passage because the problem lies within me. I do not have sufficient knowledge of electrical wiring, with all its inherent and related areas of tools, standards, materials, and procedures.

Another example of this principle was recently offered by Tierney and Pearson (1985):

> Original: The batsmen were merciless against the bowlers. The bowlers placed their men in slips and covers. But to no avail. The batsmen hit one four after another with an occasional six. Not once did a ball look like it would hit their stumps or be caught.
>
> Adaptation: The men were at bat against the bowlers. They did not show any pity. The bowlers placed their men in slips. They placed their men in covers. It did not help. The batsmen hit a lot of fours. They hit some sixes. No ball hit the stumps. No ball was caught.

No matter what adjustments are made according to readability formulas, this passage will be inaccessible to readers unfamiliar with cricket.

Educational psychologist David Ausubel (1968, p. vi) once said, "The single most important factor influencing learning, is what the student already knows." Frank Smith, in Chapter 5 of his book *Essays into Literacy* (1983), elaborates on the idea that nothing is comprehended if it does not reflect or elaborate on what the reader already knows.

In earlier publications Smith (1975, 1982) has discussed the compromise or trade-off that exists between the visual and nonvisual information that the brain sifts through during the act of reading. With little background knowledge, the reader is forced to rely heavily on visual cues. Unfortunately, the brain is severely limited in the amount of visual information that can be processed at any one time, making comprehension slow and tedious. On the other hand, a reader who can recall a wealth of previous information about the topic will be required to sample far less of the acutal printed material to comprehend the passage.

Roney (1984) takes the idea of background experience even further, saying that the concept includes a reader's understanding of print, language functions, the usefulness of reading, and the story structure.

Roney's comments bring us to the third area of schema research, *formal schema* or the knowledge of the rhetorical patterns in which information is presented. Familiarity with the way in which information is usually given affects the speed at which readers can process the passage. The following example illustrates the point: Simply ask anyone to name the 12 months of the year in 30 seconds in alphabetical order. I have never met anyone who is capable of correctly naming more than five or six months in the time allotted. The problem is that we are used to dealing with this set of items in only one way, chronologically. Trying to process or use them in any other way presents a difficult task for the brain.

Likewise, readers who are familiar with narrative structures in their culture may not be able to efficiently process different narrative structures in another culture or language.

The results of a number of studies (Kintsch & Van Dijk, 1975; Mandler & Johnson, 1977; Meyer, 1975, 1979; Meyer & Rice, 1982; Johnson & Mandler, 1980; Rumelhart, 1975, 1980) reveal that stories have a schematic structure and that readers are sensitive to it and use it in processing and recalling the events of a story. We know that different cultures organize thoughts differently. We are all familiar with Kaplan's now famous article in which he describes graphically the various patterns of rhetoric that are used in a number of cultures (Kaplan, 1966).

For a while, people were questioning whether any of this had anything to do with reading in a second or foreign language. Clarke (1980) argued that the reading skills of good L1 readers are not transferred to their reading in a foreign language, due, most likely, to the linguistic limits of the readers.

Carrell (1983b) has also demonstrated that readers in a foreign language apparently do not access previous knowledge in the processing of new material as is done when reading in their native language.

However, there have been a number of studies that have since suggested that reading in a second language involves the same processes as reading in the first language. The first was Hudson (1982), who examined Clarke's short-circuit theory and went on to show that teaching relevant knowledge to the students beforehand allowed them to override, to a great extent, their linguistic limitations. In several recent articles, Carrell (1983c, 1984a, 1984b), in a further refinement of her research design, has also shown that readers do indeed employ both content and formal schema in the process of reading in a second language.

The question that remains is: How can we, through the use of our understanding of the three above-mentioned areas of the reading process, improve our instruction, selection and/or creation of reading material, and thereby our students' comprehension?

It appears that teachers have a responsibility to provide students with the prior knowledge or experience they will need to read efficiently and with understanding. It seems that the instruction that a teacher provides before students read is more important than what that teacher does afterwards.

Reading Material

Research tells us that students may fail for several reasons:

1. They don't have the appropriate formal schema to match.
2. They aren't familiar with the content or topic.
3. They may have the wrong perception or a different perception of the ideas being presented.

What characteristics seem to help students improve their reading strategies and comprehension?

James and Evans (1984) discussed some of the primary concerns with the reading texts currently on the market both for first and second language situations. The first concern was for the variety of the readings. This would appear ironic since most publishers list variety as one of the advantages of their new readers. In any typical reader, we are aboard the space shuttle one day, the day after examining the roles of men and women in Luxembourg, or the following day in the bloodstream watching red blood cells turn blue. L1 texts are typically more varied in content than L2/ESL texts, though this will cease to be a major distinction for long, given the current trend to model ESL readers more and more after L1 materials.

According to schema research, the more you know, the more you can learn. Does this variety really provide needed background information? Schema theory indicates the answer is No. This was not the reasoning for the variety in the first place. In most cases the variety is built in to interest the readers, to "turn them on" to reading. With such variety, it is hoped, each student will find something interesting at least once during the year.

However, by forcing students to constantly be reading about the unseen, the remote, and the bizarre, we deprive them of the use and development of one of a good reader's prime strategies: top-down processing. This process is useless when reading about something that is completely outside the experience (whether personal or vicarious) of the reader. Forced to take the information in bit by bit, the reader automatically slows down, and by so doing, reinforces a bad habit—carefully reading word by word.

In a related study, Johnson (1981) demonstrated that the cultural origin of a story had more of an impact than the semantic and syntactic complexity of the text itself. Her group of Iranian students, for example, had the same comprehension scores for an adapted version of an American folktale as they did for the original.

Since the key to learning is to play upon what the learner already knows, it would seem logical that L2 readings be about a somewhat familiar or narrower area. In summary, variety can be destructive, without focus or foundation.

Several authors and scholars have recommended the use of narrow reading, possibly with the use of local materials, such as school newspapers, local novels, and so forth (Carrell & Eisterhold, 1983; Krashen, 1981). This is a way for the teacher to work with the diversity in the class, because the necessary background information can be fairly well controlled.

It might be argued that one cannot read about one subject for the entire year. A suggestion would be to create a number of thematic units, perhaps one for each week. Not one reading, as is often the case, but a unit with plenty of readings.

Another mistake that we often make is that of drilling a passage into the ground with close scrutiny to each sentence, grammar point, and vocabulary item. A large body of research has focused on this issue, with a slight majority of the studies agreeing that extensive reading is superior to intensive reading. Extensive does not mean the reading of everything under the sun, but the quantity of time spent reading about the same or related topics. A fine example would be a novel, perhaps even an adapted one. Better to have read six romance novels than to have parsed every sentence in a famous classic short story. Constant close attention to detail does not reinforce the global skills schema-theoretical research claims are crucial to efficient reading and comprehension.

Another severe limitation in the nature of most ESL reading texts is passage length. If it is true that incoming information triggers an existing knowledge structure, it would seem that shorter does not necessarily mean simpler. Often texts are so short that it is a wonder students ever get their top-down processing running smoothly before the text is finished. In addition, adaptations sometimes take out the natural redundancy that provides clarity and a certain amount of fluency for the reader. Given the maxim that the more you learn the more you can learn, shorter certainly does not mean better.

Another point that needs to be made here is that we often fail to make a connection between what we do in class and what we all do outside the class. Students often begin to perceive reading or a particular skill as an end unto itself. Our students should get the idea that good readers always relate what they already know (their schemata) to the reading task at hand. However, because of the poor or bizarre nature of the reading material, this principle may not occur to many students nor often be possible.

Brooks, Dansereau, Spurlin, and Holley (1983) make one suggestion for those who are interested in writing their own materials. The results of this study on the influence of subtitles and outlines on comprehension and recall indicate that embedded subtitles were very helpful but outlines were not. These embedded subtitles were only useful when the students were explicitly instructed concerning their presence and purpose. For developmental and L2 reading situations, this type of organizational reminder is quite effective, assuming the teacher spends a little time introducing it. The study indicates the necessity and possibility of improving students' awareness and use of formal schema for comprehension and recall through explicit instruction.

The Prereading Phase

With better materials in hand, we are ready to look at what a teacher should do before actually letting the students read. What a person already knows affects comprehension; therefore, what we do as teachers before our students attack the reading will greatly affect the results of their efforts. The better we prepare our students, the better the results will be.

The two primary goals of prereading activities should be (a) to bring to consciousness the tools and strategies that good readers use when reading, and b) to provide the necessary context for that specific reading task. (Beatie, Martin, & Oberst, 1984).

Several studies have attempted to look at how we can prepare students to comprehend the reading. One activity that does not seem to help, despite widespread use, is prereading vocabulary exercises. It apparently does not help to have students "take care of" possible unfamiliar words before reading. Though the exercise may help in vocabulary development, it does not significantly improve overall comprehension (Hudson, 1982; Johnson, 1982). In fact, according to Johnson, the vocabulary study seemed to result in a word-by-word reading approach which, as already mentioned, is detrimental to comprehension.

There are several approaches that do help. One of these is semantic webbing, explained by Freedman and Reynolds (1980). In this approach, teachers graphically connect the various concepts and key words surrounding a particular topic on the blackboard, helping students to clearly see the possible relationships between the ideas being discussed.

Schema research tells us why this works. We are not necessarily creating new knowledge in the students but simply making students aware of that knowledge that they do have—consciousness raising of a sort. We are giving structure to content knowledge that will enable them to associate what they are learning with what they already know.

Another successful activity has been student discussion. One such method is called prep or pre-reading plan (Langer, 1981). First the teacher writes what comes to the minds of the students when certain words are mentioned. Then the instructor asks the students what made them say what they said. This second step allows for introspection, further refinement, or correction.

Then the ideas are organized in a relational or hierarchical structure much like an outline or a webbing. There is a particular advantage to student-generated discussion and that is the opportunity the teacher has to assess the level of familiarity that the class in general, and each student individually, possesses.

Another related procedure that has been used with second language learners in public schools is called the *direct reading-thinking activity* (Arlington Public Schools, 1981). This procedure involves three steps: prediction, reading, and confirmation. From the title of the story, students brainstorm about topics and related ideas. The teacher then allows the students to read a portion of the passage silently. Upon completion, students are given an opportunity to alter their predictions if necessary. When they finish the passage they confirm their predictions about the story by marking or reciting the relevant portions.

Another type of prereading activity is questioning. Instead of giving questions after the reading, teachers should give them before, so that the task more closely reflects what happens in the real world. We most often read to find the answer to a question, to find information relating to a certain topic, or simply to confirm what we already thought we knew to be true.

Wilhite (1983) discusses the influence of questions on students' comprehension. Prepassage questions by their very nature induce a selective attention strategy. Teacher-generated questions tend to have a debilitating effect on student comprehension because students begin to search for the answers to the detriment of their processing of the reading. You cannot blame students for their strategy given the fact that their grade often depends more on their ability to answer the questions than on their ability to comprehend the story.

The question remains—what kind of questions will best aid comprehension as a whole? Wilhite (1983) concludes that low-level questions induce low-level recall and high-level questions concerning superordinate ideas and concepts allowed for higher-level processing without any detriment to recall of the low-level details. He posited that the higher-level questions created structures for associating a good number of the lower-level ideas, while any number of lower-level questions did not result in the formulation of higher-level structures of recall. Wilhites and Rickards and Denner (1978) show that this strategy (prequestioning) is useful only for less-skilled readers. It appears that the better one reads, the less one needs this kind of prompting.

Miriam Chaplin (1982) talks about student-generated questions. Chaplin proposes that students generate their own questions before they read, again in an effort to more closely match instruction with what happens in the real world. In a related article, Henry (1984) discusses the various ways he goes about eliciting student-generated questions. Taking this a step further, Chaplin points out that the students should then have to revise their questions after the reading and submit them, instead of the answers, confirming the popular saying, "It's not knowing the right answer that's important but knowing how to ask the right questions."

Bransford and Johnson (1972) showed that something as simple as a title creates a significant difference in students' comprehension. In other words, sometimes a title or key word is enough to get students thinking before they read. We have seen many text books that require students to read a passage. They are then asked the following question: Which would be the best title for this reading? Choose from the answers a, b, c, or d. Perhaps this strategy is a good testing device, but I do not think this kind of question teaches anything and therefore does not belong in a textbook or in a classroom exercise.

Bransford and Johnson's research says one more thing that we ought to remember when writing our own materials. Do not make up cute but mysterious-sounding titles. Professional conventions encourage presenters to make the title informative and to the point. In the case of our students, the title should allow them to start focusing immediately and accurately on the general topic of the reading.

One caution that should be made here is that simply inducing the students' previous knowledge structures may not be enough. As mentioned earlier, if the reader's schema does not match with the incoming data, one of two things can happen. The reader must choose to change that perception or to reject the data. In a study of third graders by Lipson (1984), the poorer readers at that level tended to reject the incoming data in favor of their own preconceived notions whether they were right or wrong. Results of developmental readers, of course, must be interpreted with caution with regard to developing L2 readers.

Minorities and second language learners only multiply the possibility of misconceptions, contrasting points of view and experiences that will lead them to make false assumptions and conclusions about the material they are reading. This would hold true for both content and formal schemata. Different cultures have different ways of organizing their thoughts and rhetoric as many studies have confirmed.

Of particular interest at this point is a study by Anderson, Pichert, and Shirley (1983) which highlights the influence a teacher has on the performance of students. The research indicated that students could be induced to remember different ideas from a reading depending on what information or point of view the teacher gave them before the reading. Not only that, but given a different point of view after the first test of recall, the subjects were able to recall other details about the topic that had not previously been accessible.

The Postreading Phase

When the student is finished reading, what should we do? First of all, many of the principles discussed concerning the nature and role of prereading questions apply to questioning in the postreading phase.

Wixson (1983) points out that different questions produce different kinds of output; questions should be chosen that will require the student to focus on the desired concepts. Even with post-questions alone, low-level questions tend to produce low-level processing, and vice versa with high-level questions.

However, studies concerned with story grammar, such as Lalas (1983), have indicated that simply having a fair share of higher-level questions is not enough. For some time it was popular to model the postreading phase questions after Benjamin Bloom's Taxonomy of Educational Objectives (1956). Certainly this was an improvement for many of our texts, but Lalas points out that this type of questioning is still only a means of testing, rather than teaching, comprehension. Questions should be ordered according to the events of the story in order to facilitate the proper processing and recall of the story or exposition. Math tables are not taught by jumping around from place to place. They are approached systematically. When finished, we then take sample problems out at random to test the students' mastery of the tables.

One further caution concerning the nature of the questions was raised by McConaughy (1982). Simply stated, children at different ages are at different stages of cognitive development and maturity in their story schema development and thus cannot be expected to answer the same type of questions as adults. Questions should be sensitive to cognitive stages of development, first identifying explicit events and actions of the story, as they are the most salient to young children and then more implicit concepts such as character reactions, feelings, plans and so forth.

In summary, it must be said that we have spent too much time on postreading activities, and as a result, have only been testing our students. The key to instruction, it would seem, is in the prereading stage. Tierney and Pearson (1985) make eight suggestions for improving classroom practices. At the top of the list is, "Be sure to find out your students' prior knowledge of the topic and text genre before beginning to read." In light of schema-theoretical research, the idea of "getting off on the right foot" takes on new meaning. Instruction and preventive medicine have always been more successful than postmortem examinations in improving one's health. The same applies to reading. No amount of instruction can compensate for actual reading, but, with intelligent selection and preparation, we can make our students' reading more efficient, and ultimately, more enjoyable.

References

Anderson, R. C., Pichert, J. W., & Shirey, L. L. (1983). Effects of the reader's schema at different points in time. *Journal of Educational Psychology, 75,* 271-279.

Arlington Public Schools. (1981). *Primary ESOL program, K-3* (Available from Arlington Public Schools, 1426 North Quincy Street, Arlington, VA).

Ausubel, D. P. (1968). *Educational psychology: A cognitive view*. New York: Holt, Rinehart, and Winston.

Beatie, B. A., Martin, L., & Oberst, B. (1984). Reading in the first-year college textbook: A syllabus for textbook authors, publishers, reviewers and instructors. *The Modern Language Journal, 66*, 203-211.

Bloom, B. (1956). *Taxonomy of educational objectives*. New York: Longmans, Green & Co.

Bransford, J. D., & Johnson, M. K. (1972). Contextual prerequisites for understanding some investigations of comprehension and recall. *Journal of Verbal Learning and Verbal Behavior, 1*, 717-726.

Brooks, L. W., Dansereau, D. F., Spurlin, J. E., & Holley, C. D. (1983). Effects of headings on text processing. *Journal of Educational Psychology, 75*, 292-302.

Carrell, P. L. (1983a). Background knowledge in second language comprehension. *Language Learning and Communication, 2*, 25-34.

Carrell, P. L. (1983b). Three components of background knowledge in reading comprehension. *Language Learning, 33*, 183-207.

Carrell, P. L. (1983c, November). *The effects of rhetorical organization on EFL/ESL readers*. Paper presented at the Second Language Research Forum, University of Southern California, Los Angeles.

Carrell, P. L. (1984a). Evidence of a formal schema in second language comprehension. *Language Learning, 34*, 87-112.

Carrell, P. L. (1984b). The effects of rhetorical organization on ESL readers. *TESOL Quarterly, 18*, 441-469.

Carrell, P. L., & Eisterhold, J. C. (1983). Schema theory and ESL Reading Pedagogy. *TESOL Quarterly, 17*, 553-573.

Chaplin, M. T. (1982). Rosenblatt revisited: The transaction between reader and text. *Journal of Reading, 26*, 150-154.

Clarke, M. (1980). The short circuit hypothesis of ESL reading—or when language competence interferes with reading performance. *The Modern Language Journal, 64*, 203-209.

Freedman, G., & Reynolds, E. (1980). Enriching basal reader lessons with semantic webbing. *The Reading Teacher, 33*, 677-684.

Henry, R. (1984). Reader-generated questions: a tool for improving reading comprehension. *TESOL Newsletter, 18*, 29.

Hudson, T. (1982). The effects of induced schemata on the short circuit in L2 reading: Non-decoding factors in L2 reading performance. *Language Learning, 32*, 1-31.

James, M., & Evans, N. (1984, March). *ESL reading texts and reading comprehension: Bridging the gap*. Paper presented at the 18th Annual TESOL Convention, Houston.

Johnson, P. (1981). Effects on reading comprehension of language complexity and cultural background of a text. *TESOL Quarterly, 15*, 169-181.

Johnson, P. (1982). Effects on reading comprehension of building background knowledge. *TESOL Quarterly, 16*, 503-516.

Johnson, N. S., & Mandler, J. M. (1980). A tale of two structures underlying and surface forms in stories. *Poetics, 9*, 51-86.

Kaplan, R. B. (1966). Cultural thought patterns in inter-cultural education. *Language Learning, 16*, 1-20.

Kintsch, W., & van Dijk, T. A. (1978). Toward a model of text comprehension and production. *Psychological Review, 85*, 363-394.

Krashen, S. (1981). The case for narrow reading. *TESOL Newsletter, 15*, 23.

Lalas, J. (1983). Story grammar application in ESL reading. *TESL Reporter, 16*, 67-71.

Langer, J. A. (1981). From theory to practice: A prereading plan. *Journal of Reading, 25*, 152-156.

Lipson, M. Y. (1984). Some unexpected issues in prior knowledge and comprehension. *The Reading Teacher, 27*, 760-764.

McConaughy, S. H. (1982). Developmental changes in story comprehension and levels of questioning. *Language Arts, 59*, 580-589.

Mandler, J. M., & Johnson, N. S., (1977). Remembrance of things parsed: Story structure and recall. *Cognitive Psychology, 9*, 111-151.

Meyer, B. J. F. (1975). *The organization of prose and its effects on memory.* Amsterdam: North Holland.

Meyer, B. J. F. (1979). Organizational patterns in prose and their use in reading. In M. L. Kamil & A. J. Moe (Eds.), *Reading research: Studies and applications* (pp. 109-117). Clemson, SC: National Reading Conference.

Meyer, B. J. F., & Rice, G. E., (1982). The interaction of reader strategies and the organization of text. *Text, 2*, 155-192.

Rickards, J. P., & Denner, P.R., (1978). Inserted questions as aids to reading text. *Instructional Science, 7*, 313-346.

Roney, R. C. (1984). Background experience is the foundation of success in learning to read. *The Reading Teacher, 38*, 196-199.

Rumelhart, D. E. (1975). Notes on a schema for stories. In G. Bobrow & A. Collins (Eds.), Representation and understanding: Studies in Cognitive science. New York: Academic Press.

Rumelhart, D. E. (1980). Schemata: The building blocks of cognition. In R. J. Spiro, B.C. Bruce, & W. E. Brewer (Eds.), Theoretical issues in reading comprehension (pp. 33-38). Hillsdale, NJ: Lawrence Erlbaum Associates.

Smith, F. (1975). *Comprehension and learning.* New York: Holt, Rinehart, and Winston.

Smith, F. (1982). *Understanding reading (3rd ed.).* New York: Holt, Rinehart, and Winston.

Smith, F. (1983). *Essays into literacy.* London: Heinemann Educational Books.

Thelen, J. (1982). Preparing students for content reading assignments. *Journal of Reading, 25*, 544-549.

Tierney, R. J., & Pearson, P. D., (1985). New priorities for teaching reading. *Learning*, 14-17.

Wilhite, S. C. (1983). Pre-passage questions: The influence of structural importance. *Journal of Educational Psychology, 75*, 234-244.

Wixson, K. (1983). Postreading question-answer interactions and children's learning from text. *Journal of Educational Psychology, 30*, 413-423.

Conclusion

In the introduction to this anthology, Patricia Carrell identifies a number of general integrative themes around which the individual studies, for all their particular differences, tend to cluster. These include one overarching megatheme, the notion of reading as "a multifaceted, complex, interactive process which involves many subskills and many types of reader as well as text variables." Specific subthemes include (a) the need for employing many different kinds of research approaches to a process as varied and complex as reading, (b) the role of bottom-up and top-down processing skills and the interplay between them, (c) the relationship between reading skill and general language proficiency, (d) the special importance of culturally determined background knowledge, and finally (e) the differences between reading in a first and in a second language. This conclusion explores the implications of these themes both for further research and for the teaching of second-language reading to our students.

Given the obvious complexity of the conception of reading as an interactive process involving many kinds of reader variables (e.g., background knowledge, processing strategies) and text variables (e.g., cultural assumptions, linguistic density), it should be obvious that researchers will have to continue to employ a wide range of approaches, ranging from statistical analyses of texts to such person-oriented techniques as interviews, introspections, and think-aloud protocols if we are ever to develop a fuller understanding of the process as a whole. For teachers it seems equally obvious that no one method of teaching is likely to emerge as consistently best for every combination of reader and text in every possible setting, which suggests that the good reading teacher must develop a repertoire of useful methods and procedures and a sense of what, in a particular setting, is likely to work best for different kinds of readers. (For specific suggestions, see Nuttall, 1982; Dubin, Eskey, and Grabe, 1986.)

Less obvious, but equally important, is the fact that a process as complex as reading cannot be broken into a series of steps that a teacher can take into a classroom and teach. Like other cognitive functions, reading is one that the normal human brain is preprogrammed to master, but readers must acquire this useful ability for themselves. The teacher's role is to facilitate, not to control, that acquisition process. The teacher must eventually develop a sense of what can and cannot be taught in reading classes and must learn to define the teaching role as one of creating conditions within which students can develop their inherent potential for becoming readers of a second language— each to the best of his or her abilities.

For researchers, the question of the extent to which reading is simply a function of general language proficiency (i.e., is language dependent) and the extent to which it is a specific cognitive skill, more dependent on general background knowledge and the use of sound text-attack strategies than on linguistic knowledge or decoding skills, will remain a major issue for many years to come. It is clear that top-down processing skills which focus on the meaning, not the forms, of text play a major role in all successful reading, as in relating new information from the text to background knowledge as an aid to comprehension and to creating plausible expectations for the text. It does not follow that such skills can in any way obviate the need for simple bottom-up language processing skills, and at the moment we know depressingly little about the way in which these two kinds of skills merge in reading, or the extent to which more reliance on one kind can sometimes compensate for weaknesses in the other. (For discussion of this issue, see Stanovich, 1980; Weber, 1984; for discussion in a second language context, see Clarke, 1979, 1980.) For teachers, the major implication of all this is that the wise teacher will steer a middle course between the Rudolf Flesches who believe that reading is merely linguistic decoding, and top-down enthusiasts who believe that any well-informed reader, armed with the proper top-down strategies, can read any second language text, no matter what the level of its language. It is clear that for a given second language reader, any of these general areas of concern—knowledge of the language, cultural and conceptual background knowledge, and the use of appropriate reading strategies—may become a major problem. The well-prepared teacher will be equipped to deal with whatever kind of problem the student is having, the current status of theories and models notwithstanding.

In second language learning as a whole these days, the question of the extent to which first and second language learning are alike or different has become a major issue, and second language reading is no exception to this trend (see Devine, 1981; Connor, 1984). Researchers whose subjects are second language readers must work with one eye on vast bodies of research on first language readers, much of which may be relevant to their concerns. (Singer & Ruddell, 1985, provide an excellent recent summary.) However, questions remain: What research is relevant or most relevant? And to what degree? In the years to come, such researchers must try to distinguish between what is universal in the reading process and what is peculiar to the second language reader. For the teacher with some knowledge of the research involved, the operational question becomes: To what extent will first and second language readers respond to similar approaches (for the teacher with mixed classes, this is a real-world issue) and to what extent do second language readers represent special problems which call for different kinds of instruction? One clear example of the latter situation which the studies in this volume identify is the problem of cultural background knowledge in reading. Clearly, readers with a cultural background that is different from that of a writer whose text they must read will require more extensive preparation for reading that text and others like it, regardless of their general knowledge of the language, than a reader of similar background would require. An awareness of such issues should be of real use to teachers in selecting and adapting texts for second language readers, and in preparing those readers to deal with the texts selected (Hudson, 1982; Carrell & Wallace, 1983; Carrell, 1984).

In relation to the major theme of this book, reading as a complex, interactive process, there is, for the teacher of second language reading, one final implication worth noting. Although it may be true that any speaker of a first or a second language can acquire some degree of proficiency in reading, to develop such a complex, multifaceted skill to any meaningful extent requires intensive practice over time with increasingly more challenging kinds of texts. If, in other words, teachers really hope that their reading classes will result in students who can read well in the language of the course, they must devote a good deal of thought to the problem of how to get the students reading in sufficient quantity to assure that meaningful improvement can occur. Since interest is the key to motivation in reading, this entails guiding students to appropriate materials and then providing both opportunities and incentives to read. For younger readers, this might mean anything from the comics to the works of Judy Blume; for adults, it might mean anything from the want ads to readings related to academic majors. In all of these cases one principle remains. Unless students can somehow be induced to develop a serious interest in some kind of reading that leads to a long-term reading habit, all talk of teaching reading becomes meaningless (cf. Krashen, 1985). There is much that can be done to help students along, and to wean them from counter-productive strategies, but providing appropriate material to read, that is, material which the students themselves find interesting or useful at a level which is largely comprehensible to them, should always be the teacher's first priority. The informed reading teacher will quickly come to realize that the product of good reading instruction must be readers, readers for whom such instruction constitutes just one brief stop on the way to a lifetime of reading.

To sum up, it should be noted that although this anthology does exemplify the wide range of issues and research approaches that is characteristic of research in reading in English as a second language, it also, and equally, exemplifies those themes that tend to draw this wide-ranging body of research together, both for the researchers and for informed classroom teachers. Whatever our differences in focus or approach, we can recognize a number of similar needs: the need to maintain a diversity both in research and in teaching appropriate to the complexity of the total reading process; the need to better understand the interplay between bottom-up and top-down processing in reading; the need to specify the similarities and differences between reading in a first and in a second language; and, finally, the need to define more precisely what it means to teach reading to students of English as a second language. To the extent that the collection of studies in this volume moves us closer to fulfilling this central cluster of needs, it will have made its contribution to the theory and practice of second language reading as a unified field.

David E. Eskey

References

Carrell, P. L. (1984). The effects of rhetorical organization on ESL readers. *TESOL Quarterly, 18,* 441-469.
Carrell, P. L., & Wallace, B. (1983). Background knowledge: Context and familarity in reading comprehension. In M. A. Clarke & J. Handscombe (Eds.), *On TESOL '82* (pp. 295-308). Washington, DC: TESOL.
Clarke, M. A. (1979). Reading in Spanish and English: evidence from adult ESL Students. *Language Learning, 29,* 121-150.
Clarke, M. A. (1980). The short-circuit hypothesis of ESL reading—or when language competence interferes with reading performance. *Modern Language Journal, 64,* 203-209.
Connor, U. (1984). Recall of text: Differences between first and second language readers. *TESOL Quarterly, 18,* 239-256.
Devine, J. (1981). Developmental patterns in native and non-native reading acquisition. In S. Hudelson (Ed.), *Learning to read in different languages.* Washington, DC: Center for Applied Linguistics.
Dubin, F., Eskey, D. & Grabe, W. (Eds.). (1986). *Teaching second language reading for academic purposes.* Reading, MA: Addison-Wessley.
Hudson, T. (1982). The effects of induced schemata on the "short circuit" in L2 reading: Non-decoding factors in L2 reading performance. *Language Learning, 32,* 1-31.
Krashen, S. D. (1985). The power of reading. In S. D. Krashen, (Ed.), *Inquiries and insights.* (pp. 89-113). Haywood, CA: Alemany Press.
Nuttall, C. (1982). *Teaching reading skills in a foreign language.* London: Heinemann Educational Books.
Singer, H. & Rudell, R. B., (Eds.). (1985). *Theoretical models and processes of reading.* Newark, DE: International Reading Association.
Stanovich, K. (1980). Toward an interactive-compensatory model of individual differences in the developmental of reading fluency. *Reading Research Quarterly, 16,* 32-71.
Weber, R. (1984). Reading: The United States. *Annual Review of Applied Linguistics, 4,* 111-123.